Verbal Reasoning Handbook

Alison Primrose

Contents

Introduction

What is an 11+ verbal reasoning exam?	4
How to use this book	6

Sorting words

1	Identify groups of words	7
2	Sort words into categories	10
3	Find words that do not belong	12
4	Find words that have letters in common	15
5	Apply alphabetical order	18

Making words

6	Find letters that finish one word and begin the next	21
7	Find a word hidden in a sentence	26
8	Add the missing letters to make a synonym of a given word	28
9	Add the missing letters to make an antonym of a given word	29
10	Make new words by adding or removing letters	31
11	Move a letter to make new words	33
12	Change letters to make new words	35
13	Find the word that completes a word	37
14	Solve anagrams	38
15	Use a rule to create new words	43

Word meanings

16	Find words that are closest in meaning	50
17	Find words that are opposite in meaning	55

| 18 | Find synonyms and antonyms | 58 |
| 19 | Words with multiple meanings | 60 |

Selecting words

20	Combine two words to make a new word	62
21	Rearrange words to make a sentence	67
22	Rearrange words to find an unnecessary word	68
23	Select the best words to make a complete sentence	69
24	Complete word analogies	72

Maths, sequences, coding and logic

25	Code using numbers, letters and symbols	76
26	Logic problems	81
27	Letter-coded sums	88
28	Complete the sum	89
29	Related numbers	90
30	Number sequences	95
31	Letter sequences	98
32	Letter analogies	101
33	Complete crosswords	105

Skills builder

Verbal reasoning at home	108
Out and about verbal reasoning	109
Learning and practising verbal reasoning skills	110

Study guide	111
Glossary	114
Answers	116

Introduction

What is an 11+ verbal reasoning exam?

Verbal reasoning is a test that uses words and numbers to show logic and reasoning. It is a common test for the 11+ exam. Success in verbal reasoning requires a thorough understanding of the English language with its associated rules and patterns, excellent spelling skills and a wide-ranging vocabulary.

The 11+ exam is taken by children at the beginning of Year 6. It is a test used by state-funded grammar schools or by selective schools for Year 7 onwards. It is used to select the children who perform the best under exam conditions and to place them in a school environment with peers of a similar academic ability. Unlike most other exams, selective entrance tests cannot be retaken. There is no second chance at the 11+ (although some schools do still set exams for entry at 12+ or 13+), so there is often fierce competition to perform well and achieve good results.

There is one main exam board involved in producing 11+ verbal reasoning exams: Granada Learning (GL) Assessment. There are other exam boards and individual schools who write their own papers and some schools will have the 11+ exam completed on a computer rather than on paper.

An 11+ verbal reasoning paper can be written in two formats, following either a multiple-choice or standard layout. For a multiple-choice paper, children will need to choose their answer from a set of options and mark it on a separate answer sheet. Answers must be marked in these booklets very carefully as the answer sheets are often read and marked by a computerised system. In the standard format, children must write each answer directly onto the question paper.

As with most exams, 11+ exam papers are timed, typically lasting between 45 minutes and one hour. The introduction of a time-limit can potentially have an impact on a child's performance, so it is important for children to work through practice materials in both timed and non-timed environments.

The scope and content of an 11+ verbal reasoning test can often differ across UK regions, as there is a range of question types that can be included. However, a paper will generally be intended to test a child's ability to:

- process verbal information
- apply logical thinking and problem-solving skills
- find and follow patterns and rules
- determine word meaning
- spell accurately

- apply basic maths skills (for GL Assessment papers)
- work systematically.

These skills are tested through a series of questions that include:

Sorting words

This is the ability to identify groups of words and to place them into categories. Other questions include finding words that do not belong in a group, placing words in alphabetical order and recognising words with letters in common.

Making words

This section covers a wide variety of skills and tests the ability to understand how words are made by moving, changing, adding or removing letters. It also includes finding hidden words and missing letters as well as using a rule to create new words. Spelling is tested through problems involving anagrams.

Word meanings

The question types in this section test the ability to identify words that are most similar and most opposite. Vocabulary knowledge is tested through a range of questions, including finding words with multiple meanings.

Selecting words

This is the ability to choose words that combine to make new words. Sentence structure is tested through tasks that involve rearranging words in sentences and identifying unnecessary words. The ability to understand and solve word analogies is also covered in this section.

Maths, sequences, coding and logic

This is the ability to work out letter and number sequences and to code and decode words using numbers, letters or symbols. Questions also include letter-coded sums, discovering number relationships and making deductions from given information.

This book will help you to understand the key questions found in verbal reasoning exams. The Bond range of verbal reasoning assessment papers and the CEM English and verbal reasoning books can be used alongside this book to apply the information. Bond also offers a range of exam test papers in both multiple-choice and standard format.

How to use this book

The book has been divided into sections. How you work through the book is up to you. You can choose to work through the sections in order and complete the questions within them sequentially. Or if you prefer, you can choose any section to start and pick and choose a particular question type within that section.

Each numbered section includes an explanation of the particular question type and the skills that you will need to be able to answer the questions. Make sure you read through all the information carefully before attempting any questions and ask a parent or helper if you do not understand.

Example boxes

For each question type, one or more examples are provided to show you the suggested way to work through the questions and to aid your understanding.

Example boxes look like this:

Have a Go questions

These questions give you the opportunity to check your understanding of what you have just learned. For some of the longer questions, you might find it easier to do your working out on some spare paper.

HAVE A GO

In each section you will also find useful **Exam Tips** and important information that you should try to **remember** and apply when working through the questions both in practice sessions and in the actual test itself.

Glossary

Throughout the book important words and phrases that commonly occur in verbal reasoning test questions are included. You will find definitions of these words and phrases in the glossary at the end of the book. The glossary terms have been highlighted in black bold the first time that they appear in each section.

> **TOP TIP!**
> It's a good idea to have access to a dictionary whilst working through verbal reasoning questions in this book so that you can look up new words that you meet and write down their definitions.

A note on question formats

The majority of 11+ exams now use multiple-choice answer format (where you choose your answer from a list of options). In Bond practice materials, some questions are multiple-choice and some require you to write or type the answer into a box, known as 'standard format'. We continue to use both because standard format questions are proven to be more effective for learning and practise, as having to decide on an answer yourself and the simple act of writing out your answer, make your brain work a bit harder and helps those important skills to get fixed in your memory, ready to be used when you sit down for the real test.

We hope you enjoy using the book. Good luck!

Sorting words

There are five different question types within the sorting words category:

- identify groups of words
- sort words into categories
- find words that do not belong
- find words that have letters in common
- apply alphabetical order.

What skills do I need?

- a broad **vocabulary**
- the ability to spot connections between different words
- knowledge of word classes, including **nouns**, **verbs** and **adjectives**
- careful checking
- sound knowledge of the alphabet.

❶ Identify groups of words

You may be asked to sort words into existing groups. In order to do this, you will need to work out the common theme that links all the words in a group together. You may be able to think of more than one thing that the group has in common, so make sure you try out all of your ideas as the answer may not be the first thing you consider!

Here is an example.

Look at these groups of words.

A	B	C	D
car	table	bread	stomach
bus	bookshelf	pancake	liver
lorry	stool	pizza	brain

Choose the correct group for each of the words below.
Write in the letter.

1 pasta _____   2 bench _____   3 sofa _____
4 heart _____   5 lungs _____   6 van _____

Sorting words   7

Sorting words

Here are some of the links that the words have in common:

A	B	C	D
vehicles	pieces of furniture found in the home	types of food made from wheat	parts of the body internal organs

Having identified these common themes, it should be easy to put each new word into the right group:

1 pasta **C**
(food)

2 bench **B**
(furniture)

3 sofa **B**
(furniture)

4 heart **D**
(internal organ)

5 lungs **D**
(internal organ)

6 van **A**
(vehicle)

HAVE A GO

1 Look at these groups of words.

A	B	C	D
cow	violin	tea	potato
horse	trumpet	wine	leek
elephant	drums	lemonade	cabbage

Choose the correct group for each of the words below.
Write the letter on the line.

coffee _____   piano _____   mouse _____

onion _____   flute _____   tiger _____

Here is another similar question type, where you are looking for a common link between a set of words.

Look at this example:

> **Underline the word in the brackets that goes best with the words given.**
>
> word, paragraph, sentence   (pen, cap, letter, top, stop)

Carefully read the words given outside the brackets. Think about what they have in common:

- They are all to do with writing.

AND

- They are all elements that make up a piece of writing.

Which word in the brackets also has these links in common?
Work through them one by one:

pen	cap	letter	top	stop
↓	↓	↓	↓	↓
NO	NO	YES	NO	NO
Used for writing but not an element of a piece of writing.	Nothing to do with writing.	You write a letter to someone. AND it is an element of a piece of writing.	Nothing to do with writing.	You may think of a full stop but 'stop' on its own is not an element of writing.

Paragraphs are made up of sentences, sentences are made up of words and words are made up of letters. **Letter** is the right answer and should be underlined.

Sorting words

HAVE A GO

2 Underline the one word in the brackets that goes best with the words given outside the brackets.

a lake, canal, ocean   (wave, rain, boat, river, cruise)

b aeroplane, jet, helicopter (cloud, glider, airport, pilot, take-off)

c plate, cup, bowl   (spoon, mug, saucer, glass, saucepan)

❷ Sort words into categories

In some questions, the links between the words will be given and you have to correctly identify the words that have these links.

Look at this example:

> Write the following words in the correct groups.
>
> wardrobe   bungalow   wood   table   mansion
>
> plastic   steel   cottage chair
>
> Buildings   Materials   Furniture
>
> _____   _____   _____
>
> _____   _____   _____
>
> _____   _____   _____

Look at each of the titles of the three groups; these show you the common links that you are looking for. Now read each word in turn and think about what it has in common with the title of each group. Here are the first three examples:

Sorting words

wardrobe	→ It is not a building. → It is not a material. → It is a piece of furniture.		wardrobe belongs in the **Furniture** group
bungalow	→ It is a one-storey building. → It is not a material. → It is not a piece of furniture.		bungalow belongs in the **Buildings** group
wood	→ It is not a building. It is a material. → It is used to make furniture → but it is not a piece of furniture.		wood belongs in the **Materials** group

This type of question relies on your knowing the words shown, so you should take every opportunity to try to widen your vocabulary, as you never know what might come up!

REMEMBER: If lines are given below the titles of the groups, this can give you a clue about how many words belong in each group.

HAVE A GO

1 Write the following words in the correct group.

tin   grasshopper   indigo   steel   beige

butterfly   scarlet   earwig   aluminium

Colours   Metals   Insects

_____   _____   _____

_____   _____   _____

_____   _____   _____

Sorting words

2 Write the following words in the correct group.

| leopard | sombrero | ferret | fez | orchid |
| rose | tulip | beret | pangolin | |

Flowers   Hats   Animals
_____   _____   _____
_____   _____   _____
_____   _____   _____

3 Write the following words in the correct group.

| eaglet | artichoke | ankle | fennel | osprey |
| knuckle | broccoli | pheasant | pupil | |

Birds   Vegetables   Parts of the body
_____   _____   _____
_____   _____   _____
_____   _____   _____

❸ Find words that do not belong

In order to answer this question type, you need to find a common theme or link between a group of words and then identify the word or words that do not have the same link.

Underline the two words that are the odd ones out in the following group of words.

black   king   purple   green   house

12 Sorting words

Look at this example:

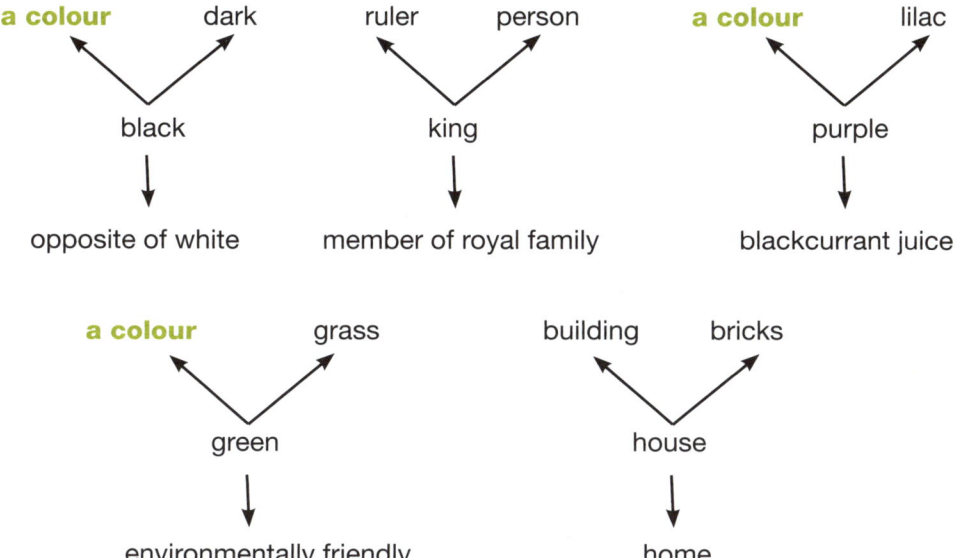

Has a common link been found between three of the words?

Yes, black, purple and green are all colours. The two odd ones out, which should be underlined, are **king** and **house**.

REMEMBER: If the link is not easy to see, note down as many things as you can think of.

HAVE A GO

1 Underline the two words that are the odd ones out in the following group of words.

May   December   Easter   Friday   August

Sometimes there is a connection between all five words and you have to look for differences in the meanings of the words that will help you to separate three of the words into a group.

Sorting words

Look at this example:

> Underline the two words that are the odd ones out in the following group of words.
>
> bang   chime   boom   jingle   crash

All five words are sounds, so we have to think about the differences between them to find the group of three. We can link bang, boom and crash together as they can all mean a loud noise, whereas chime and jingle are much quieter, more musical sounds, usually associated with the noises made by a clock or bells. Therefore, we can group together bang, boom and crash, and choose **chime** and **jingle** as the odd words out.

HAVE A GO

2 Underline the two words that are the odd ones out in the following group of words.

unicorn   lamb   dragon   cow   horse

The most challenging questions of this type require you to be able to categorise words into groups of nouns, verbs, adjectives and so on in order to find out the odd words.

Look at this example:

> Underline the two words that are the odd ones out in the following group of words.
>
> increase   contract   grow   gigantic   swell

Increase, grow, gigantic and swell all have an **association** with something large, whereas contract means to make something smaller. So contract is one of our odd words out. What is the other one?

To find out, we now have to sort the other words by categorising them as verbs, nouns or adjectives.

increase	verb and noun
grow	verb
gigantic	adjective
swell	verb and noun

By doing this, we can see that three of the words are verbs and mean to make something bigger, whereas gigantic is an adjective meaning 'huge' and doesn't mean to make something bigger. The two odd words out are therefore **contract** and **gigantic**.

> **HAVE A GO**
>
> **3** Underline the two words that are the odd ones out in the following group of words.
>
> shield   sword   defend   castle   protect

④ Find words that have letters in common

As well as being identified by their meaning, words can also be sorted according to their letters. For these questions you need to look very carefully at the letters in a word.

There are two very similar question types in this group. In the first type, you must find the word that *can* be made from the letters in the word in capitals. In the second, the word that *cannot* be made from the letters in the word in capitals must be found.

Look at this example:

> Underline the one word that can be made from the letters of the word in capital letters.
>
> C H A M P I O N   camping   notch   peach   cramp   crimp

Consider each of the words in turn, carefully checking its letters against those in the given word – CHAMPION in this example. Are all of the letters available to make each of the other words?

The correct answer for this type of question will give a '✓' by each letter.

C	A	M	P	I	N	G	
✓	✓	✓	✓	✓	✓	✗	camping *cannot* be made
N	O	T	C	H			
✓	✓	✗	✓	✓			notch *cannot* be made
P	E	A	C	H			
✓	✗	✓	✓	✓			peach *cannot* be made
C	R	A	M	P			
✓	✗	✓	✓	✓			cramp *cannot* be made
C	H	I	M	P			
✓	✓	✓	✓	✓			chimp **can** be made

REMEMBER: If the same letter appears twice in the given word in capitals, it can be used twice in the other words.

The answer is **chimp** as all of its letters are contained in the word CHAMPION.

HAVE A GO

1 Underline the one word that can be made from the letters of the word in capital letters.

P E R S P E C T I V E   viewer   perceive   creature   prevent   protect

The same process can be used to find which word *cannot* be made using the letters of the given word in capitals.

> Underline the one word that cannot be made from the letters of the word in capital letters.
>
> S T A T I O N E R Y   stone   tyres   ration   nation   noisy

Follow the same method as described above to find the answer in this version.

In this example you will find that **nation** cannot be made as it needs two letter 'n's and there is only one 'n' in STATIONERY.

REMEMBER: As these two question types are so similar, it is very important that you read and follow the instructions precisely.

HAVE A GO

2 Underline the one word that cannot be made from the letters of the word in capital letters.

U N D E R G R O U N D   dungeon   undone   grudge   order   dodge

Sorting words

There is a third question type that also involves looking at the letters in words. In these questions, you have to identify words that are made up of the same letters.

Again, you need to work carefully, letter by letter.

Look at this example:

> Underline the two words that are made from the same letters.
>
> TAP   PET   TEA   POT   EAT

Working from left to right, compare the letters of each word with the letters in the words to its right.

T A P compared to: **P** E **T**   **T** and **P** the same but no A in PET

                      T E **A**   **T** and **A** the same but no P in TEA

                      P O **T**   **T** and **P** the same but no A in POT

                      E **A T**   **T** and **A** the same but no P in EAT

Repeat the process with the second word:

P E T compared to: **T E** A   **E** and **T** the same but no P in TEA

                      P O **T**   **P** and **T** the same but no E in POT

                      E A **T**   **E** and **T** the same but no P in EAT

Sorting words 17

Continue comparing all of the options until you find the answer.

Following this clear step-by-step process, you can see that the answer to this example is **TEA** and **EAT**. They both consist of the letters T, E and A.

> ### HAVE A GO
>
> **3** Underline the two words that are made from the same letters.
>
> TILES   ITEMS   TRIES   MILES   TIMES

⑤ Apply alphabetical order

This question type tests your knowledge of the alphabet and your ability to place words and letters in alphabetical order. The questions require a secure knowledge of the alphabet, careful observation skills and **logical** thinking.

Don't worry if you do not know the meaning of some of the given words – you don't need to know what they mean in order to answer this type of question.

Let's look at two examples of questions based on alphabetical order.

> If the letters in the following word are arranged in alphabetical order, which letter comes in the middle? Write the letter on the line.
>
> EXTRAVAGANT _____

The simplest way to solve this type of question is to number each letter of the word in alphabetical order starting with the first 'a', which is given the number 1.

So we can number the letters of EXTRAVAGANT like this:

4	11	8	7	1	10	2	5	3	**6**	9
E	X	T	R	A	V	A	G	A	**N**	T

As there are 11 letters in the word, the middle letter will be letter 6, which is **N**.

REMEMBER: Write out the alphabet on rough paper if you prefer to read it as you work through alphabetical order questions.

Sorting words

> **HAVE A GO**
>
> **1** If the letters in the following word are arranged in alphabetical order, which letter would be in the ninth position? Write the letter on the line.
>
> GRASSHOPPER _____

Now Look at this example:

> If these words were placed in alphabetical order, which word would come fourth? Underline the word.
>
> anxiety   auction   ancient   axiomatic   auxiliary

Work carefully from left to right, looking at each letter in turn.

If you write out the words in a grid, it will make the letter ordering easier to follow.

	1	2	3	4	5	6	7	8	9
1	A	N	X	I	E	T	Y		
2	A	U	C	T	I	O	N		
3	A	N	C	I	E	N	T		
4	A	X	I	O	M	A	T	I	C
5	A	U	X	I	L	I	A	R	Y

- Column 1 shows us that each word begins with an **A**. This does not help with the reordering, so move on to column 2.
- Column 2 shows that two words have a second letter **N**, two words have a second letter U and one word has a second letter **X**. As N comes before U and X in the alphabet, you should first compare the two words with an N in rows 1 and 3 (anxiety, ancient).
- In rows 1 and 3, column 3 shows the letters **X** and **C**. As C comes before X in the alphabet, it is clear that the first word is ANCIENT. The second word must be ANXIETY.
- Now look at the two words that have a U as the second letter in rows 2 and 5 (auction, auxiliary). Column 3 shows that the third letters for these words

Sorting words 19

are a **C** and an **X**. The letter C comes before X in the alphabet so the third word is AUCTION and the fourth must be AUXILIARY.
- This leaves the word in row 4, AXIOMATIC, as the fifth word.
- The reordered table, showing the five words in alphabetical order, looks like this:

	1	2	3	4	5	6	7	8	9
1	A	N	C	I	E	N	T		
2	A	N	X	I	E	T	Y		
3	A	U	C	T	I	O	N		
4	A	U	X	I	L	I	A	R	Y
5	A	X	I	O	M	A	T	I	C

It is now easy to identify the fourth word in the list:

AUXILIARY (in the fourth row).

If the question asks you which word would be in a particular position if the words were put in reverse alphabetical order, follow the process above and then work up from the bottom of the reordered grid to find the answer.

REMEMBER: Always read the question very carefully so the different variations do not catch you out!

You can also use this method if the question asks for the alphabetical order when the words are written backwards. Just remember: start with the *last* letter of each word, not the first!

HAVE A GO

2 If these words were placed in alphabetical order, which word would come third? Underline the word.

surname   surveys   survive   surgeon   surplus

3 If these words were written backwards and then placed in alphabetical order, which word would come fifth? Underline the word.

dentist   against   calmest   combust   amongst

Making words

There are twelve question types in this group:

- finding letters that finish one word and begin the next
- find a word hidden in a sentence
- add the missing letters to make a **synonym** of a given word
- add the missing letters to make an **antonym** of a given word
- make new words by adding or removing letters
- move a letter to make new words
- change letters to make new words
- find the word that completes a word
- solve **anagrams**
- find the three missing letters to complete a word
- find the missing letters to complete words in a paragraph
- use a rule to create new words.

What skills do I need?

- good knowledge of the alphabet including vowels and consonants
- understanding of how words are constructed
- good spelling
- knowledge of root words
- careful observation and a **logical** approach
- ability to work out a rule or connection and apply it to new words.

❻ Find letters that finish one word and begin the next

This type of question tests your spelling skills as well as your **vocabulary** knowledge and can be presented in different ways.

Your task is to choose a letter or letters that will finish the first word and begin the second word.

Look at this example:

> Find the letter that will end the first word and start the second word.
>
> p e a c (_____) o m e

You may be able to think of the missing letter straight away, just by looking at the letters that are given. But don't worry if you can't.

One of the easiest ways to tackle this type of question is to use your knowledge of the alphabet. Go through each letter of the alphabet in turn, adding it to the end of the first group of letters. Ask yourself these questions each time:

If the answer is 'yes' to both of these questions, write the word down and try the letter in front of the second group of letters. Then ask yourself the same two questions. When the answer is 'yes' to both these questions again, that letter is the answer.

So, the above example can be worked through like this:

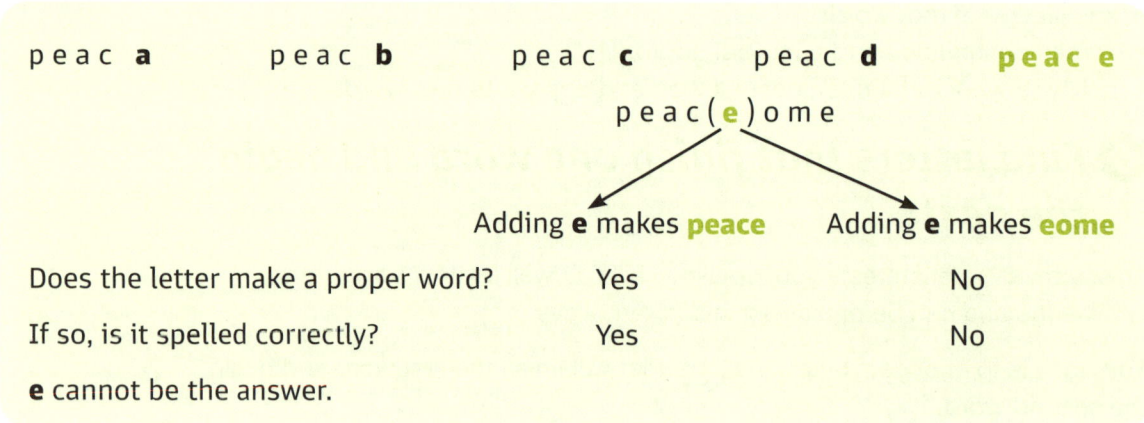

Continue working through the alphabet:

peac f   peac g   **peac h**

peac(**h**)ome

Adding **h** makes **peach**   Adding **h** makes **home**

Does the letter make a proper word?	Yes	Yes
If so, is it spelled correctly?	Yes	Yes

h is the missing letter.

HAVE A GO

1 Find the letter that will end the first word and start the second word.

g r a s (_____) e o p l e

In this next example, you have to find the letter that will finish the first word and begin the second word of each pair.

Find the letter that will complete both pairs of words, ending the first word and starting the second. The same letter must be used for both pairs of words.

m e a (_____) a b l e   f i (_____) u b

Making words 23

This example can be worked through as follows:

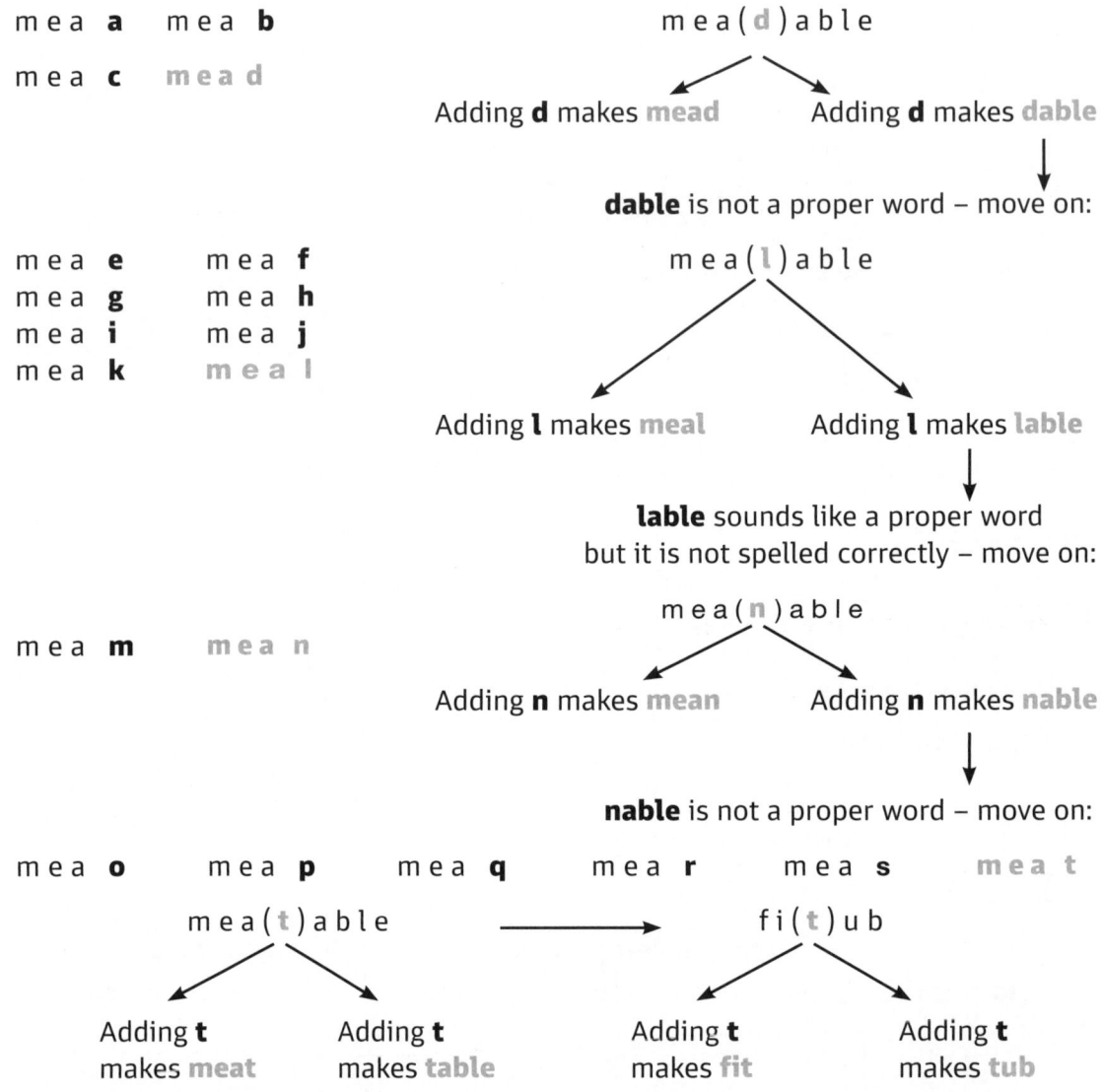

This letter makes four proper words that are spelled correctly, so the answer is **t**.

HAVE A GO

2 Find the letter that will complete both pairs of words, ending the first word and starting the second. The same letter must be used for both pairs of words.

s i g h (_____) w i s t   s t a r (_____) r a p

More challenging questions of this type require you to find a pair of missing letters.

Look at this example:

Find two letters that will end the first word and start the second word.

r e a (_____ _____) a i r

Knowing letter pairs that are frequently used to start and finish words is an effective tool to use with this more advanced question type. Here is a list of some common letter pairs, many of which start with a **vowel**:

ad al am an ap ar as at aw

ed el em en er

ic id im in ir is it

ob on or ot ow

un ur us ut

be ce de fe ge le me ne pe re se te ve we

ch sh th

st sp

With a word that begins 'rea', it's unlikely that the next letter will be another vowel, so let's look at the letter pairs that consist of two **consonants**.

If we add 'ch' to the end of the first word, we can make the word 'reach'. Placing 'ch' in front of 'air' makes 'chair'.

The letters 'ch' make two proper words and are therefore the correct answer.

REMEMBER: If you find it easier to find the beginning of words rather than the end, you can start with making the second word first.

HAVE A GO

3 Find two letters that will end the first word and start the second word.

t r a v (____ ____) e c t r i c

7 Find a word hidden in a sentence

This question type requires you to look at the individual letters in words closely and use them to find hidden words in a sentence. Your vocabulary knowledge and spelling skills are also tested as you need to be able to recognise the hidden terms as proper words when you find them.

Look at this example:

> Find the four-letter word hidden at the end of one word and the beginning of the next word. The order of the letters may not be changed. Underline the word.
>
> The children had bats and balls.

The question tells you that the word you are looking for is hidden at the end of one word and the start of the next one. If you break the sentence down into two-word sections, you can make sure that you check every gap between the words.

The word has four letters so, working carefully from left to right, check each group of four letters spanning each gap. Ask yourself if the four letters make a proper word each time.

REMEMBER: If you have difficulty focusing on just four letters, use your fingers to cover up the other letters as you read from left to right.

Following this process, the example would be solved like this:

The children ✗
The children ✗ No proper word between these two words.
The children ✗

child**ren h**ad ✗
child**ren ha**d ✗ No proper word between these two words.
child**ren had** ✗

had bats ✗
had bats ✗ No proper word between these two words.
had bats ✗

bats **a**nd ✗
bats **an**d ✗ The word **SAND** is made
bats **and** ✓ between these two words.

and balls ✗
and balls ✗ No proper word between these two words.
and balls ✗

The answer is **sand**: The children had bat**s and** balls.

HAVE A GO

Find the four-letter word hidden at the end of one word and the beginning of the next word. The order of the letters may not be changed. Underline the word.

a Try to be as polite as your brother.

b He put the ingredients into a blender.

c Would you like to watch our performance?

d The vase toppled over and shattered.

8 Add the missing letters to make a synonym of a given word

This question type tests your skills in spelling and your knowledge of vocabulary. It can be in multiple-choice or standard format. The example below is in multiple-choice format: it offers a range of possible answers. In standard format, these possible answers don't appear.

Look at this example:

> The following word has some letters missing. Complete the word by selecting the missing letters from options A–E to make a word that has a similar meaning as the word on the left.
>
> pretty   b _____ a _____ t _____ f u _____
>
> A e a i l   B e t f l   C e u i l   D e u a t   E l s r l

Here is an effective step-by-step technique to use with this question type.

1 Try to think of a word that means the same as 'pretty' and begins with 'b'. Write the word, then cross out the given letters and match the remaining letters.
2 If you can't recognise the word straight away, you need to look at the options. There is not sufficient time to write out every word with every combination, so try to narrow them down:
   - Think of common spelling strings. It is common for words to end in 'ful', so reject any letter groups that do not end in 'l'. This means option D can be rejected.
3 Which options are left? Try writing them out and choose which looks right:
       A beaatiful   B beattfful   C b**eu**ti**l**   E blastrful

Option C (**e u i l**) has the correct spelling.

HAVE A GO

The following words have some letters missing. Complete the words by selecting the missing letters from options A–E to make a word that has a similar meaning as the word on the left.

a MUTE   s___e___c___le___s

   A p a k s   B p e h d   C s o n e   D p e h s   E u e h n

b BRAVE   c o___r a___e o_____

   A u d e s   B u g u s   C p g l d   D u g e s   E r s n d

c MENACING   s_____i s___e___

   A i n r t   B a r t r   C i n d t   D u p r t   E i n t r

9 Add the missing letters to make an antonym of a given word

This question type tests your skills in spelling and your knowledge of vocabulary. It can be in multiple-choice or standard format.

The example below is in standard format, which means that no possible answers are suggested. (In multiple-choice format, there would be different possible answers to select from.)

Look at this example:

The following word has some letters missing. Complete the word to make a word that has the opposite meaning to the word on the left.

sunset   

Making words

Follow this step-by-step process to solve these questions.

1. See if you can recognise the word straight away from the given word and the letters. What does 'sunset' mean? It means the start of darkness when the sun is going down. What word means the opposite of 'sunset' and begins with 's'?
2. If you cannot recognise the word, look at where the vowels and consonants fall. The second letter must be a vowel because there would not be another consonant between 's' and 'n'. This gives us 'san', 'sen', 'sin', 'son', 'sun' or 'syn' at the beginning of the word. 'Sun' is the most likely beginning to the word as this relates to the time of day.
3. Think of common spelling strings, for example:
   - It is common for words to end in 'ase', 'ese', 'ise', 'ose', 'use' or 'tse'.
   - After the 'n' the most common consonants would be d, f, g, k, l, m, n, p, r, s, t.
4. Read through the letter groups you have to see if you can find a word. Work logically through each option until you find a suitable word.

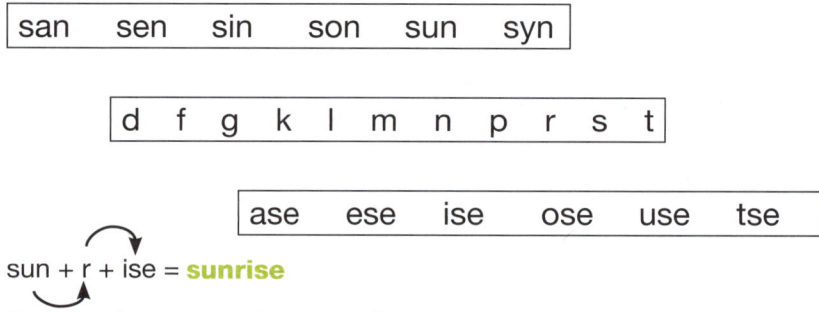

sun + r + ise = **sunrise**

Sunrise has a meaning opposite to sunset.

HAVE A GO

The following word has some letters missing. Complete the word to make a word that has the opposite meaning to the word on the left.

a flawed   p ____ r ____ e ____ t

b intentional   a ____ c ____ d ____ n t ____ l

c natural   ____ r t ____ f i ____ i a ____

10 Make new words by adding or removing letters

In some **verbal reasoning** questions, you are asked to make new words by either adding letters to a given word or removing letters from it. These questions test spelling skills. It is helpful to learn basic spelling rules in preparation for these – and to check up on frequently used **exceptions**.

In the first type, you have to select a letter to add to the beginning of all the given words, making new, proper words out of each of them.

Look at this example:

> Which one letter can be added to the front of all of these words to make new words? Write the letter on the line.
>
> _____ are   _____ at   _____ rate   _____ all

Start by working through the alphabet in your mind, adding each letter in turn to the front of the first word. When you find a letter that works, test it with the second word and so on, until you find a letter that makes four proper words.

aare   NO

bare   YES   **b**at   YES   **b**rate   No

care   YES   **c**at   YES   **c**rate   YES   **c**all   YES

We have made four proper words, so the correct letter to add is **c**.

HAVE A GO

1 Which one letter can be added to the front of all of these words to make new words? Write the letter on the line.

   a   _____ing   _____ait   _____hale   _____ave

   b   _____ite   _____nown   _____nife   _____ettle

Not all missing letters can be added at the beginning of a given set of words. In some questions, the letters may be added anywhere within the word and, for these questions, you cannot follow the same simple process using the alphabet.

Making words

As there may be several possible positions for a missing letter, sometimes a clue will be given to help you find the correct letter and make the required word.

Look at this example:

> Add one letter to the word in capital letters to make a new word. The meaning of the new word is given in the clue. Write the new word on the line.
>
> PLAN   simple   _____

As the extra letter may be added anywhere in the word, it is easier to start with the clue.

What synonyms can you think of for the clue?

What other words do you associate with it?

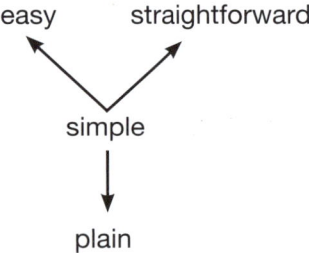

Once you have noted down your ideas, check each one against the word in capital letters. Can one of these words be made by adding one letter to the given word in capitals?

In this example, 'plain' is clearly made by the addition of an 'i' to the word 'plan', so **plain** is the answer.

HAVE A GO

2 Add one letter to the word in capital letters to make a new word. The meaning of the new word is given in the clue. Write the new word on the line.

    a   SHOE   beach   _____

    b   RUSH   squash   _____

Now look at this variation, where you need to take away a letter instead of adding one in order to find the answer.

> Remove one letter from the word in capital letters to make a new word. The meaning of the new word is given in the clue. Write the new word on the line.
>
> AUNT   an insect   _____

With this question type, there are only a limited number of letters that can be removed; just four in the case of this example – A, U, N and T. You can therefore follow a process of elimination to find the answer.

Working from left to right, remove each letter in turn and check at each stage if a proper word has been made. If it has, check that its meaning matches the clue. Remember that there may be more than one word that can be made by removing one letter, but only one will be related to the clue.

A̶UNT   UNT   not a word

AU̶NT   ANT   yes, a word and an insect, so ANT is the answer

AUN̶T   AUT   not a word

AUNT̶   AUN   not a word

REMEMBER: Always check the other options once you think you have got the answer as there may be an even better option.

HAVE A GO

3 Remove one letter from the word in capital letters to leave a new word. The meaning of the new word is given in the clue. Write the new word on the line.

a   HAUNT   search   _____

b   SCALE   deal   _____

11 Move a letter to make new words

This question type is very similar to the previous question type, and it also tests vocabulary knowledge and spelling skills. As with many other verbal reasoning question types, you need to use a logical approach to find the answers.

Making words

In the first example of this type, you need to remove one letter from the first word and add it to the second word. You must make sure that you have made two new proper words and that they are spelled correctly.

Look at this example:

> Move one letter from the first word and add it to the second word to make two new words. Write both words on the lines.
>
> hunt   sip   _____   _____

The easiest way to find the answer is to work carefully through the first word from left to right, removing each letter in turn. Use the point of your pencil to cover up each letter in the word on the left in turn. Does it leave a word? In the example above, the only letter that can be removed and still leave a proper word is 'n'.

When the remaining letters make a proper word, try the letter removed in all possible positions in the second word to see if a new word can be created.

$$\text{sip} + \text{n}$$

	Put the letter 1st	Put the letter 2nd	Put the letter 3rd	Put the letter 4th
	n s i p	s n i p	s i n p	s i p n
Proper word?	✗	✓	✗	✗

In this example, the two new words are **hut** and **snip**.

HAVE A GO

Move one letter from the first word and add it to the second word to make two new words. Write both words on the lines.

a crack   rumble   _____   _____

b grill   tip   _____   _____

c yearn   led   _____   _____

d sight   sag   _____   _____

12 Change letters to make new words

In this question type, you are changing letters in either two or three steps to create a new word. If you follow a similar careful process and ask yourself the same types of questions, you will find the right answer.

Look at this example:

> Change the first word into the last word, by changing one letter at a time and making a new, different word in the middle. Write the answer on the line.
>
> CASE   _____   LASH

CASE has to be able to change into LASH in two steps. The new word you have to make will form the first step in the sequence.

First, notice which letters in the first word are different from the last word.

C A S E ____ A S ____ L A S H

Only one of these letters can be changed at a time. Which one will form a new word that can then be changed into LASH? Let's take each letter in turn.

Step 1

CASE   **L**ASE   LASH   LASE sounds like a proper word but it is not spelled correctly.

CASE   CAS**H**   LASH   CASH is a proper word spelled correctly.

Double-check that this is the correct answer by working through the second step in the sequence.

Step 2

CASE   CASH   **L**ASH   This step also works. The correct answer is **CASH**.

HAVE A GO

1 Change the first word into the last word, by changing one letter at a time and making a new, different word in the middle. Write the new word on the line.

COST   _____   FAST

Making words

Making words

Sometimes this question type appears with two blanks in the middle. This means the first word will change into the last word in three steps and you must find the words that form the first two of these steps. Although this variation is a little more difficult, you can still use the same process to work out the answers.

Look at this example:

> Change the first word into the last word, by changing one letter at a time and making two new, different words in the middle. Write the new words on the lines.
>
> TEAK _____ _____ RENT

As before, note down which letters in the first word are different from the last word.

TEAK

RENT

Only one of these letters can be changed at a time. Which one will form the first new word?

Step 1

Try changing each letter in turn:

TEAK	**R**EAK	**REAK** is not a proper word.
		The T cannot be the first letter to change.
TE**A**K	TE**N**K	**TENK** is not a proper word.
		The A cannot be the first letter to change.
TEA**K**	TEA**T**	**TEAT** is a proper word spelled correctly.
		The K must be the first letter to change.

Step 2

Work through the next step: **TEA**T

RENT

TEAT	**R**EAT	**REAT** is not a proper word.
		The T cannot be the next letter to change.
TE**A**T	TE**N**T	**TENT** is a proper word spelled correctly.
		The A must be the second letter to change.

Making words

Step 3

Check the last step: **T**ENT   Yes – changing the T to R gives the final

RENT   required word, spelled correctly.

The sequence is correct. The answers are **TEAT** and **TENT**.

> **HAVE A GO**
>
> **2** Change the first word into the last word, by changing one letter at a time and making two new, different words in the middle. Write the new words on the lines.
>
> a CLIP _____   _____ PLAY
>
> b SCARF _____   _____ SPACE

13 Find the word that completes a word

To solve this question type, you need to understand how words relate to each other in order to create meaning in sentences. Your ability to recognise **context** and your spelling skills are also tested by this type of question.

Look at this example:

> Find the three-letter word that can be added to the letters in capitals to make a new word. The new word will complete the sentence sensibly. Write the three-letter word on the line.
>
> The MO scampered across the room. _____

The rest of the sentence is your clue, so try reading the sentence without the incomplete word to see if you can work out what the missing word needs to be.

In the example above, the clue is in the word 'scampered'. This helps you to think about animals that scamper. Now use the letters that you have been given to help you identify the correct animal. The first two letters of the word are MO. Once you think you know the missing word, try writing it out, taking care with spelling.

An animal that scampers, with the first two letters of its name being MO, is a mouse.

M̶O̶ U S E

Crossing through the first two letters leaves us with the word **USE**, which is a whole word and therefore the correct answer.

HAVE A GO

Find the three-letter word that can be added to the letters in capitals to make a new word. The new word will complete the sentence sensibly. Write the three-letter word on the line.

a The pony TTED across the yard. _____

b I POLID my shoes until they shone. _____

c The teacher NED the class that the test would be difficult. _____

d At the monster-themed party, the children wore MS. _____

14 Solve anagrams

To solve **anagrams**, you need to rearrange a given set of letters to make a proper word that will complete the sentence.

Look at this example:

> Rearrange the muddled letters in capitals to make a proper word. The answer will complete the sentence sensibly. Write the word on the line.
>
> A BEZAR is an animal with stripes. _____

You may be able to see the proper word straight away but, if you can't, this step-by-step process will help you find the answer.

1 Read the sentence carefully saying the words in your head and leaving a blank in the place of the jumbled-up word (anagram).

   A _____ is an animal with stripes.

Making words

38 Making words

2 Note down any striped animals that you know and compare the letters they consist of with the letters of the anagram. You may find it helpful to make notes in a table.

Striped animals?	Using letters BEZAR?
tiger	✗
badger	✗
zebra	✓

A **zebra** has stripes and is made up of the letters **BEZAR**, so it is the correct answer.

HAVE A GO

1 Rearrange the muddled word in capitals to make a proper word. The answer will complete the sentence sensibly. Write the word on the line.

The photographs brought back many happy SEMRMIOE. _____

Sometimes there are two jumbled words in a sentence. Again, it is the context, the clues from the meaning of the other words, that will help you to work out the anagrams.

Look at this example:

Rearrange the muddled words in capital letters so that the sentence makes sense. Write the words on the lines.

There are sixty SNODCES in a UTMINE. _____ _____

The clue here is the word 'sixty' – what things are connected with sixty?

MINUTES	**SECONDS**	**DEGREES**
There are **sixty minutes** in an hour.	There are **sixty seconds** in a minute.	There are **sixty degrees** in the angles of equilateral triangles.

Making words

Making words

Look at the letters in the words you have thought of and the letters in the anagrams.

Are there any that match? Yes.

SNODCES → SECONDS

UTMINE → MINUTE

The correct answer should read:

There are sixty **SECONDS** in a **MINUTE**.

> **REMEMBER:** When reordering letters in anagrams, it can be helpful to cross through letters as you use them. This way you can see clearly which letters are left to fit into the word.

HAVE A GO

2 Rearrange the muddled words in capital letters so that the sentence makes sense. Write the words on the lines.

DNELYDSU there was a loud NGBA. _____ _____.

To be able to answer the third type of anagram question, you will need good knowledge of word meanings and synonyms.

Look at this example:

> Rearrange the letters in capitals to make another word. The new word has something to do with the first two words. Write the word on the line.
>
> spot   soil   TASNI   _____

To find the correct answer, you must first work out the connection between the two words on the left. Think about the meaning of each word:

a place, location ↖   ↗ a mark, **stain**   earth, mud, ground
                  spot   ↕
                                                       soil
to see or notice something ↙   ↘ a pimple   to make dirty, **to stain** something

What common link can you find between the two words? They are both to do with making something dirty or staining something.

Now look again at the word in capitals. It is made up from the letters TASNI.

STAIN is a synonym of both spot and soil and consists of the same letters as TASNI.

Stain must be the correct answer.

> ### HAVE A GO
>
> **3** Rearrange the letters in capitals to make another word. The new word has something to do with the first two words. Write the word on the line.
>
> power   strength   GRNEYE   _____

More challenging types of anagram questions, where good spelling is very important, ask you to find a letter that is missing from two words whose letters have been scrambled.

Look at this example:

> **In the sentence below, two words in capitals have had one letter removed and their remaining letters mixed up. The same letter has been removed from both words. Write the missing letter on the line.**
>
> **The weather is HRTOE in summer than in NWRIE.   ____.**

Remember to focus first on the context of the sentence. In this example, the sentence is about seasons and weather changes. You may be able to unscramble the second word first to find the word WINTER and see that the missing letter is **T**. Going back to the first word, you can now unscramble the letters and add the letter T to reveal HOTTER.

In this type of anagram question, it is not essential to unscramble both words as the letter missing is the same in each word.

Making words

HAVE A GO

4 In the sentence below, two words in capitals have had one letter removed and their remaining letters mixed up. The same letter has been removed from both words. Write the missing letter on the line.

I told my best NFERI that I was afraid of RESPIS. _____

Another variation of this question type involves adding a letter to a word to make a new word that fits with the given description.

Look at this example:

Add one letter to the word in capitals and then rearrange the letters to make a new word that fits the description. Write the new word on the line.

MATE   groups of people who work together   _____

Keeping the description of the word that you need to make in your head, look at the letters in the word MATE and try rearranging them in a different order.

We can make new words MEAT and TEAM with the letters. By adding an 'S' to TEAM we can make **TEAMS**, which fits the description of groups of people who work together.

EXAM TIP

In an exam, you may not always get clues to an anagram. Working out all the possible options can take time, so work smart. Our eyes see words in a straight line reading from left to right, so put your letters in a circle. This forces your eyes to begin with different letters and to see combinations of **vowels, consonants, prefixes, suffixes** or common **letter strings** much more easily.

HAVE A GO

5 Add one letter to the word in capitals and then rearrange the letters to make a new word that fits the description. Write the new word on the line.

COWS   frown   _____

15 Use a rule to create new words

These questions test your ability to work out a connection or rule and then apply it to new words. The rule may relate to actual letters used, vowels and consonants, letter order or the sequence of letter strings.

The first question type is straightforward because you are given the rule.

Look at this example:

> Which word in the group contains letters from only the first six letters of the alphabet? Underline the word.
>
> defeat   farce   abide   **deaf**   dice

Start by saying the first six letters of the alphabet in your head – a, b, c, d, e, f.

Now you can scan each word and use a simple process of elimination, letter by letter, to find the answer. You might find it helpful to cross out the letters as you go through each word.

~~defea~~t	t remains
~~fa~~ r ~~ce~~	r remains
~~ab~~ i ~~de~~	i remains
~~deaf~~	all letters have been **eliminated**
~~d~~ i ~~ce~~	i remains

REMEMBER: Once you have identified one of the letters used as not being in the first six in the alphabet, you can eliminate those words straight away and move on.

The word **deaf** is the answer as it is made up from letters that occur only in the first six letters of the alphabet.

HAVE A GO

1 Which word in the group contains four vowels? Underline the word.

quiet   alone   house   audio   sauce

In the next two question types, you have to work out the rule for yourself, so you need to look carefully at the examples given. Following a clear step-by-step process is an effective way of solving these question types.

Making words

Making words

Look at this example:

> Change the first word of the third pair in the same way as the other pairs to give a new word. Write the word on the line.
>
> bind, hind   bare, hare   but, _____

1 Look at the first pair of words. How is the second word different from the first one?

bind
↓   The first letter changes from a 'b' to an 'h'.
hind

2 Test this change against the second pair:

bare
↓   The first letter changes from a 'b' to an 'h'.
hare

3 Apply the same rule to the third word to complete the third pair:

but
↓   The first letter changes from a 'b' to an 'h'.
hut

Applying the same rule to the third word makes a new proper word – the answer is **hut**.

HAVE A GO

2 Change the first word of the third pair in the same way as the other pairs to give a new word. Write the new word on the line.

mast, mash   last, lash,   cast, _____

Sometimes there is an alphabetical rule that you need to apply when creating the third pair of words.

Look at this example:

> **Change the first word of the third pair in the same way as the other pairs to give a new word. Write the word on the line.**
>
> cool, cook   beam, bean   pass, _____

1. Look at the first pair of words. How is the second word different from the first one?

   coo**k**

   ↓ The last letter changes from an 'k' to a 'l'. The letter 'l' follows 'k' in alphabetical order.

   coo**l**

2. Test this change against the second pair:

   bea**m**

   ↓ The last letter changes from an 'm' to an 'n'.

   bea**n**

3. Apply the same rule to the third word to complete the third pair:

   pas**s**

   ↓ The last letter changes from an 's' to a 't'.

   pas**t**

Applying the same rule to the third word makes a new proper word – the answer is **past**.

HAVE A GO

3 Change the first word of the third pair in the same way as the other pairs to give a new word. Write the word on the line.

line, mine   fang, gang   balm, _____

Trickier questions of this type require you to reorder the letters of the word in the same way as in the example pairs.

Making words

Making words

Look at this example:

> Change the first word of the third pair in the same way as the other pairs to give a new word. Write the word on the line.
>
> oaks, soak   oils, soil   eats, _____

The easiest way to solve this question type is to give each letter a number and write the numbers over the tops of the letters like this:

1 2 3 4   4 1 2 3
o a k s   s o a k

You can see that the order of the numbers changes when they are written over the word 'soak'.

Now apply the same letter order to 'eats', like this:

1 2 3 4   4 1 2 3
e a t s   s e a t

The new word that you have created is **seat**.

HAVE A GO

4 Change the first word of the third pair in the same way as the other pairs to give a new word. Write the word on the line.

scared, dear   sermon, norm   kicked, _____

More challenging questions sometimes involve a letter that appears twice in the first word and you won't know which letter has been used to create the second word. When this happens, use the second pair of words to confirm which letter has been used.

Look at this example:

> Change the first word of the third pair in the same way as the other pairs to make a new word. Write the word on the line.
>
> pamper, ramp   yellow, well   boards, _____

1 2 3 4 5 6   6 2 3 1/4
p a m p e r   r a m p

We don't know whether letter 1 or letter 4 has been used to create the 'p' in 'ramp', so we have to check the second pair of words to confirm.

1 2 3 4 5 6   6 2 3 4
y e l l o w   w e l l

We can now confirm that letter 4 has been used.

1 2 3 4 5 6   6 2 3 4
b o a r d s   s o a r

The new word that you have created is **soar**.

HAVE A GO

5 Change the first word of the third pair in the same way as the other pairs to give a new word. Write the word on the line.

battle, late   fields, dies   jangle, _____

Another question type involves the middle word being made from letters used in the two words on either side. Your task is to work out the correct sequence of letters and then follow the same pattern to create the missing word.

Look at this example:

Look at the first group of three words. The word in the middle has been made from the other two words. Complete the second group of three words in the same way, making a new word in the middle. Write the word on the line.

PAIN   INTO   TOOK   ALSO   _____   ONLY

In the first group of words, the word INTO has been made by using letters from the other two words. Try the following method to work out what rule has been applied to these words.

First, number each letter in the first and third words and look at which number sequence has been used to make the word INTO:

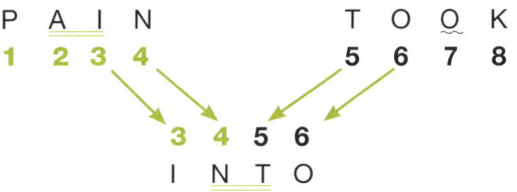

Now apply this same number sequence to the second group of words to make the new word.

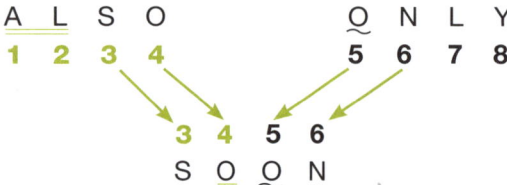

The answer to this example is **SOON**.

HAVE A GO

6 Look at the first group of three words. The word in the middle has been made from the other two words. Complete the second group of three words in the same way, making a new word in the middle. Write the word on the line.

SPIN   TOPS   TOMB   PACE   _____   TREE

This type of question can be more challenging if the first and third word in a set use some of the same letters. You need to take extra care when working through these questions, as only one number sequence will be correct.

Look at this example:

> Look at the first group of three words. The word in the middle has been made from the other two words. Complete the second group of three words in the same way, making a new word in the middle. Write the word on the line.
>
> PASTE   PALE   LEARN   COAST   _____   APPLE

As before, start with the first group of words.

PASTE   **P**ALE   **L**EARN

You can see that the letter **P** in PALE can only have come from PASTE and the letter **L** can only have come from LEARN. This shows the sources of the first and third letters of the new word.

However, there is more than one possible rule for the remaining two letters as both words have the letters 'A' and 'E'. You need to check all possible number sequences so that you can apply the correct rule.

1   Note all of the possible rules underneath the middle word.

    P A S T E   P A L E   L E A R N
    1 2 3 4 5   1 2 6 5   6 7 8 9 10
                         1 2 6 7
                         1 8 6 7
                         1 8 6 5

2   Test each one with the second group of words.

    C O A S T   ___ ___ ___ ___   A P P L E
    1 2 3 4 5   1 2 6 5   6 7 8 9 10
                         1 2 6 7
                         1 8 6 7
                         1 8 6 5

3   Match the numbers to their corresponding letters. Ask yourself if the letters make a proper word each time.

                                         A real word?
    1 2 6 5   →   C O A T   ✓
    1 2 6 7   →   C O A P   ✗
    1 8 6 7   →   C P A P   ✗
    1 8 6 5   →   C P A T   ✗

LEARN: It can help to put in the letters that you know are in the new word first – in the question above, letters 1 and 4 can be placed first.

COAT is the correct answer. It follows the same number sequence as 'PALE' and it is a proper word.

HAVE A GO

7   Look at the first group of three words. The word in the middle has been made from the other two words. Complete the second group of three words in the same way, making a new word in the middle. Write the word on the line.

    COST   TOOK   POKE   HEIR   _____   PART

Making words

Making words   49

Word meanings

There are four different question types within the word meanings category:

- find words that are closest in meaning
- find words that are the opposite in meaning
- find **synonyms** and **antonyms**
- words with multiple meanings.

What skills do I need?

- a broad **vocabulary**
- the ability to recognise synonyms and antonyms
- the ability to understand word meanings and **context**.

16 Find words that are closest in meaning

Your knowledge of words and synonyms for them – different words with very similar meanings – can be tested in a variety of ways. Having a wide vocabulary and being able to recognise synonyms are key to answering these and many other similar verbal reasoning questions.

For this first question type, you need to know the definition of a word and then look carefully to find another word with a similar meaning.

Look at this example:

> Underline the two words, one from each group, that are closest in meaning.
>
> (race, shop, start)   (finish, begin, end)

It is helpful to work **logically** from left to right when solving a question like this. So, take the first word in the first group and pair it with each of the words in the second group in turn.

Can 'race' mean finish?	No.	
or begin?	No.	
or end?	No.	'race' *cannot* be part of the answer.

Follow the same process with the second word in the first group.

Can 'shop' mean finish?   No.

or begin?   No.

or end?   No.   'shop' *cannot* be part of the answer.

So we must now be looking for a synonym for start.

Can 'start' mean finish?   No.

or begin?   **Yes**.   'start' and 'begin' have the same meaning.

or end?   No.

Underline **start** and **begin** as these are the two words that are closest in meaning.

> **REMEMBER:** Many of the words given may be linked or related in some way – but remember, you are looking for synonyms, the two words closest in meaning.

HAVE A GO

1 Underline the two words, one from each group, that are closest in meaning.

(betray, divide, knife)   (cut, share, grate)

In this second question type, you are given five words and asked to choose the two that are most similar in type or meaning.

Look at this example:

> Underline the two words that are most similar in meaning.
>
> dear   pleasant   poor   extravagant   expensive

Again, it is helpful to work from left to right, so start by reading the first word and thinking of as many different meanings as you can. What do you associate the word with?

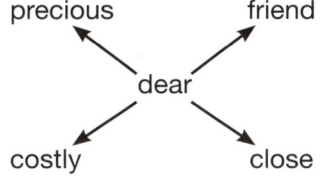

> **REMEMBER:** A thesaurus is a great help for finding synonyms.

Now read each of the other words in turn and think about their meanings in the same way.

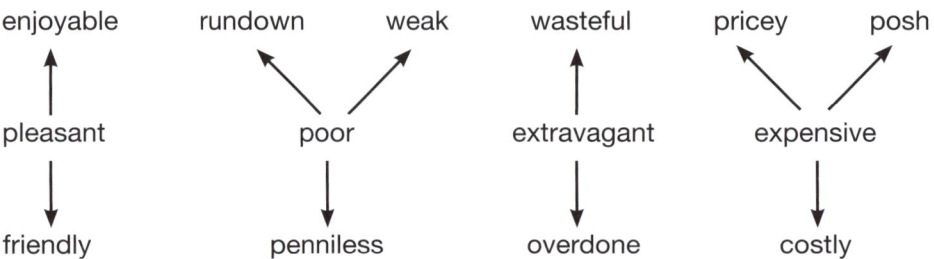

Following this thought process, it is clear that the two words with similar meanings are **dear** and **expensive**, as both mean costly.

HAVE A GO

2 Underline the two words that are most similar in meaning.

odour   attempt   review   musty   try

In another variation of this question type, you may be given a word and asked to find the best synonym from a group of words. Although the question may look different from the example above, you can still use the same thought process to find the answer.

Look at this example:

Underline the word in the brackets closest in meaning to the word in capitals.

UNHAPPY   (unkind   moody   delighted   sad   friendly)

First, consider the meaning of the given word on the left.

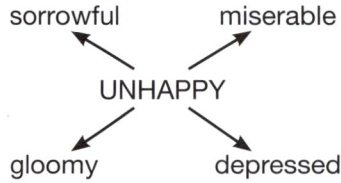

Then read through the words in the brackets to identify a synonym for this word. If it is not clear which is the best option, start working from left to right. Think about each word

REMEMBER: The tests are usually timed, so work as quickly as you can through the list of words!

in turn, noting the meaning of each one until you find the word that is closest in meaning to the word outside the brackets.

Following this logical process, you will find that **sad** is the closest in meaning to 'UNHAPPY'.

> **HAVE A GO**
>
> **3** Underline the word in the brackets that is closest in meaning to the word in capitals.
>
> GRUMBLE   (humble   curse   defy   complain   mumble)

Another similar question type requires you to look carefully at pairs of words and identify the pair of synonyms. Often, the pairs of words given in the question are linked in some way other than being synonyms. Look out for this and avoid a common mistake!

Look at this example:

> Underline the pair of words most similar in meaning.
>
> come, go   roam, wander   fear, fare

Start with the first pair and think about the meaning of each word in turn. It may help to note down what each word means.

come – arrive
go – leave

This is a pair of opposites. They are not synonyms.

roam – travel, ramble
wander – stroll, ramble

This pair of words has similar meanings.

fear – anxiety, fright
fare – fee, food, cope

These two words are spelled in a similar way but have very different meanings.

Following this process, the pair of synonyms in this example must be **roam**, **wander**.

HAVE A GO

4 Underline the pair of words most similar in meaning.

beg, plead   victory, celebrate   endure, battle

The final question type in this group draws on your knowledge of synonyms in a different way. It relies on your understanding of word definitions, but you also need your spelling and rhyming skills.

Look at this example:

> Find a word that is similar in meaning to the word in capital letters and that rhymes with the second word. Write the word on the line.
>
> CABLE   tyre   _____

Firstly, think about the meaning of the word in capitals. How many synonyms can you recall?

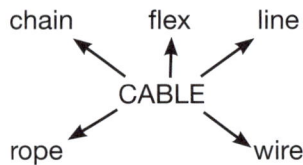

Then read through the words you have noted – do any of them rhyme with the second word?

tyre – chain? ✗   flex? ✗   line? ✗   rope? ✗   wire? ✓

Wire is the correct answer. It is a synonym for 'CABLE' and rhymes with the word 'tyre'.

REMEMBER: Rhyming words are not always spelled the same way. 'Say' the words in your head so that you can identify the sounds and see if they rhyme.

HAVE A GO

5 Find a word that is similar in meaning to the word in capital letters and that rhymes with the second word. Write the new word on the line.

REPAIR   lend   _____

17 Find words that are opposite in meaning

Words that are opposite in meaning are called antonyms. Verbal reasoning questions can also test your knowledge of words by asking for antonyms, so the wider your vocabulary, the easier you will find these questions. There are a few different ways that these questions can be presented.

Look at this example:

> Underline one word in the brackets that is most opposite in meaning to the word in capitals.
>
> WIDE   (broad   vague   long   narrow   motorway)

Think about the word outside the brackets and what it means.

Then consider each of the words in the brackets in turn, working from left to right. For each word, think about its meaning, then note down words that mean the opposite.

Do any of these antonyms include the word outside the brackets or its synonyms?

	Antonyms	wide, broad, large?
broad	narrow, thin, slender	✗
vague	precise, distinct, clear	✗
long	short	✗
narrow	**wide, broad**	✓
motorway	track, lane	✗

REMEMBER: Sometimes antonyms can be made by the addition of a prefix. For example:
un– + happy = unhappy
il– + legal = illegal
im– + patient = impatient
dis– + approve = disapprove

From these, it is clear that **narrow** is the opposite of 'wide' and so it should be underlined as the correct answer.

HAVE A GO

1 Underline one word in the brackets that is most opposite to the word in capitals.

DOUBTFUL   (rigid   lavish   expected   definite   hopeful)

Another similar question type requires you to look carefully at pairs of words and identify the pair of antonyms.

Look at this example:

> Underline the pair of words most opposite in meaning.
>
> cup, mug   coffee, milk   hot, cold

REMEMBER: These questions often include tricky alternatives, giving words that might go together but are not opposites!

For each pair, note down how the two words are related in order to identify the pair that are most opposite. Remember to work from left to right. Writing the links you think of in a table can make it easier to see the answer.

Word pair	Relationship between word pair	Opposites?
cup, mug	both containers for drinks	No.
coffee, milk	both drinks, often mixed together	No.
hot, cold	measures of different temperature values	**Yes.**

So the word pair **hot, cold** must be the answer and should be underlined.

HAVE A GO

2 Underline the pair of words most opposite in meaning.

permit, forbid   explain, rebel   seal, fasten

A third way that you may see these questions presented is when you have to choose two words that are most opposite in meaning.

Look at this example:

> Underline the two words, one from each group, that are the most opposite in meaning.
>
> (dawn, early, wake)   (late, stop, sunrise)

When the question is in this form, work through each word in the first group and think about what each word means and what its opposite might be.

REMEMBER: Check carefully that you have selected a pair of antonyms and not similar words.

Then compare the antonyms you have thought of with each of the three words in the right-hand group to find out which antonym is closest to one of the options given.

Word on left	Meaning	Antonym	late?	stop?	sunrise?
dawn	sunrise	dusk	✗	✗	✗
early	before time	late	✓	✗	✗
wake	conscious	sleep	✗	✗	✗

The words **early** and **late** are underlined as 'early' is the opposite of 'late'.

HAVE A GO

3 Underline the two words, one from each group, that are most opposite in meaning.

(careful, reckless, timid)   (gradual, cautious, childish)

EXAM TIP

If you don't know the meaning of a word but it is a multiple-choice question, see how many options you can reject so that you have fewer options to guess from. Many **nouns** do not have an opposite, but many **adverbs** and **adjectives** do. Ultimately, any guess is far better than missing out a question. Examiners don't knock marks off for wrong answers, so make sure you don't leave any gaps.

18 Find synonyms and antonyms

This question type tests both synonyms and antonyms, so like the previous two question types, it also requires a wide vocabulary. Skills in sorting through a grid of words quickly and accurately are also important.

Look at this example:

> Look at the words in the grid and then use them to answer the questions that follow. Write the answers on the lines provided.
>
> | aged | youthful | unusual | flowers | unique |
> |---|---|---|---|---|
> | astonished | terrific | elderly | young | flour |
> | rich | weak | washing | parent | grave |
> | children | flippant | yoghurt | frivolous | spine |
> | series | thought | sad | marvellous | mature |
>
> **a** Find three words that mean the same as 'old'.
>
> _____   _____   _____
>
> **b** Find two words that mean the opposite of 'serious'.
>
> _____   _____   _____

The first question asks for three words that mean the same as 'old'.

Glance through the grid to see if it is possible to immediately identify words that are linked to the word 'old', like this:

aged	**youthful**	unusual	flowers	unique
astonished	terrific	**elderly**	**young**	flour
rich	weak	washing	**parent**	grave
children	flippant	yoghurt	frivolous	spine
series	thought	sad	marvellous	**mature**

58 Word meanings

Check whether the question asks for synonyms or antonyms. (It asks for synonyms.) The words 'youthful' and 'young' are related to age, but they are antonyms for 'old', not synonyms, so they can be rejected.

Check whether you are looking for nouns or adjectives. 'Old' is an adjective, so you are looking for other adjectives. The words 'parent' and 'children' can be rejected as they are nouns.

So the correct answers are therefore **aged**, **elderly** and **mature**.

The second question asks for two words that have an opposite meaning to the word 'serious'.

A word may look or sound like another, but may mean something totally different. 'Series' looks and sounds a little like 'serious', but it has a totally different meaning, so it can be rejected. This leaves four words.

From looking carefully at all the words and thinking about their meanings, we can identify that the two words that are opposite in meaning to the word 'serious' are **flippant** and **frivolous**.

REMEMBER: If you are not sure what a word means, think back to the context in which you last heard it. For example, you may have heard a silly comment described as 'flippant' – the opposite of 'serious'.

aged	youthful	unusual	flowers	unique
astonished	terrific	elderly	young	flour
rich	weak	washing	parent	grave
children	**flippant**	yoghurt	**frivolous**	spine
series	thought	sad	marvellous	mature

Word meanings

HAVE A GO

Look at the words in the grid and then use them to answer the questions that follow. Write the answers on the lines provided.

endless	beneath	recent	tender	calculate
uncover	amazing	disclose	slender	faith
unique	depend	reliable	constant	surprise
subject	admit	radiate	affect	reveal
property	iron	softly	sincere	saturate

a Find two words that mean the same as 'continuous'.

_____   _____

b Find three words that mean the opposite of 'conceal'.

_____   _____   _____

19 Words with multiple meanings

There are many words in the English language that have more than one meaning and this forms the basis for a question type that tests your knowledge in a different way. You need to know two separate meanings of one of the options in the brackets, so you can find the right synonym for both word pairs.

Look at this example:

> Underline the one word in the brackets that will go equally well with both the pairs of words outside the brackets.
>
> rush, attack   cost, fee   (price, hasten, strike, charge, money)

Think about the meaning of the word pairs given outside the brackets. What is the common link between both words in each pair?

> rush, attack – these both mean **to move forward quickly, aggressively, forcefully**.
>
> cost, fee – these are both to do with **price, money, payment**.

Now consider the definition of each word in the brackets one at a time. Is it linked with *both* pairs? Remember the word must be linked with both pairs to be correct.

word	definition	pair	✓/✗
price	nothing to do with moving quickly	rush, attack?	✗
	cost of something	cost, fee?	✓
hasten	means to move quickly	rush, attack?	✓
	nothing to do with money	cost, fee?	✗
strike	aggressive, attacking movement	rush, attack?	✓
	nothing to do with money	cost, fee?	✗
charge	to rush forward, attack	rush, attack?	✓
	the cost or price of something	cost, fee?	✓
money	nothing to do with moving quickly	rush, attack?	✗
	relates to the cost of something	cost, fee?	✓

Charge has similar meanings to both pairs of words, so it must be the correct answer.

HAVE A GO

Underline the one word in the brackets that will go equally well with both the pairs of words outside the brackets.

a holiday, voyage   fall, stumble   (tour, slip, expedition, trip, sail)

b speck, mark   see, notice   (spot, clean, stain, observe, stare)

c basin, washbowl   descend, plummet   (bath, plunge, sink, fall, soak)

Word meanings

Selecting words

There are five question types in this group:

- combine two words to make a new word
- rearrange words to make a sentence
- rearrange words to find an unnecessary word
- select the best words to make a complete sentence
- complete word analogies.

What skills do I need?

- an understanding of how words and sentences are constructed
- good spelling
- knowledge of **root words**
- an understanding of word definitions
- careful observation and a **logical** approach.

20 Combine two words to make a new word

To solve the first question type in this group, you have to choose two words that can be put together to make another, new **compound word**.

Look at this example:

> Underline two words, one from each group, that go together to form a new word. The word in the first group always comes first.
>
> (hand, green, for)   (light, house, sure)

Work carefully from left to right. Take each word in turn from the left group and add it to each word in the right-hand group. As you read each pair of words, ask yourself the following question:

> Do these two words go together to make a new, sensible word?

hand-light	✗	
hand-house	✗	No. None of these words are sensible. The first word cannot be *hand*.
hand-sure	✗	
green-light	✗	
green-house	✓	Yes. A *greenhouse* is for plants and is made of glass.
green-sure	✗	
for-light	✗	
for-house	✗	No. None of these words are sensible. The first word cannot be *for*.
for-sure	✗	

REMEMBER: Make sure the two words you choose go together to make one new word. In the example question, you can make 'green light'. A green light often means 'go', but it is two separate words.

The two words that go together to make a new compound word are **green** and **house**.

HAVE A GO

1 Underline two words, one from each group, that go together to form a new word. The word in the first group always comes first.

   a (water, free, tide)   (sun, fall, wave)

   b (ball, deep, pass)   (kick, by, port)

In the second variation, two shorter words are combined to make one new, longer word. The short words often have a different **pronunciation** when put together to make a new word. Look carefully at the spelling of the new, longer word as well as saying it in your head.

Look at this example:

> Underline two words, one from each group, that go together to form a new word. The word in the first group always comes first.
>
> (care, be, make)   (on, am, off)

Work through each word pair as before. This time, think about the different ways the letters can be pronounced as you read the words.

care-on	✗	care-am	✗	care-off	✗
be-on	✗	**be-am**	✓	be-off	✗
make-on	✗	make-am	✗	make-off	✗

Saying the two words separately, **be** and **am**, they do not seem to make a sensible word. But if you read the letters together as one word, they make **beam**.

'Beam' is not classed as a true compound word, but it is still formed by putting two words together. Notice that the pronunciation of the whole word 'beam' does not include the separate sound of the word 'am'.

REMEMBER: If you think you have found the right answer to a question before you have finished looking through all the options, do still check the remaining words to be sure you have made the right choice! Look out for words that appear to make a compound word but are spelled incorrectly, such as MISS and LEAD which together make **MISSLEAD** instead of **MISLEAD**.

HAVE A GO

2 Underline two words, one from each group, that go together to form a new word. The word in the first group always comes first.

a (add, wars, now)   (then, here, ship)

b (so, jam, bud)   (lid, site, old)

In the third variation, you are given a set of words and you need to find one word that can be added in front of each in the set to make a new set of compound words.

Look at this example:

> Find a word that can be put in front of each of the following words to make new, compound words. Write the word on the line.
>
> CAST   FALL   WARD   POUR   _____

One of the best methods to tackle these questions is to start with a '**mind map**'. Note down as many compound words as you can think of that end with the first word on the list.

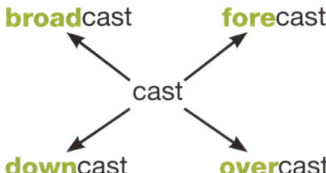

Then check the first part of each of these against the other words to see if they make new compound words, correctly spelled.

broadfall	✗	broadward	✗	broadpour	✗
forefall	✗	foreward	✗	forepour	✗
downfall	✓	downward	✓	downpour	✓
overfall	✗	overward	✗	overpour	✗

'Down' is the **prefix** that makes a new proper compound word with each of the others, so the answer is **down**.

REMEMBER: If you struggle to think of any compound words ending with the first word, you can start with any of the other words and follow the same checking process.

HAVE A GO

3 Find a word that can be put in front of each of the following words to make new, compound words. Write the word on the line.

    a WEED   SHORE   SHELL   GULL   _____

    b MARK   LET   SHOP   CASE   _____

    c SCREEN   MILL   PIPE   SURF   _____

    d PHONES   DRUM   ACHE   RING   _____

You may also be asked to find a word that can be added *after* each word in the group to make a new set of compound words.

Look at this example:

> Find one word that can go after each of these words to form five new compound words. Write the word on the line.
>
> BACK   FAIR   UNDER   PLAY   FORE   _____

As before, select one of the words to begin with. Then think of as many compound words as you can that start with that word.

For example, PLAY can be followed by: able, date, fully, group, ground, list.

Now test each of these words with the words given in the question to find the one that combines with all the words to make new, correctly spelled compound words. You can either say each word out loud to see if it sounds right or write them down.

The correct word is **ground**, which combines with the other words to make the following new compound words:

BACKGROUND   PLAYGROUND

FAIRGROUND   FOREGROUND

UNDERGROUND

HAVE A GO

4 Find one word that can go after each of these words to form five new compound words. Write the word on the line.

a HEART	DAY	WIND	OUT	TIE	_____
b BUTTER	CHEST	PEA	HAZEL	DOUGH	_____
c FIRE	HEAD	SPOT	HIGH	LIME	_____
d POWER	COUNT	POINT	WORTH	PRICE	_____

Selecting words

EXAM TIP

In an exam, you can't speak out loud, but you can sound out words in your head. Try sounding a word in different ways to see if it helps. For example, 'pig + eon' or 'fat + her' make no sense at all, but when you pronounce the words as 'pij + in' or 'fa + ther', they suddenly make a lot of sense. Another option is to quickly write the words on your question paper. Writing 'pigeon' and 'father' will then look right.

21 Rearrange words to make a sentence

This question type tests your knowledge of how to structure a sentence and your understanding of word meanings.

Look at this example:

> Find and underline the two words that need to change places to make a sensible sentence.
>
> She went to letter the write.

1 Read the sentence through quickly to get its meaning. You may automatically change the places of two words to make it make sense.

Reread, going through slowly, stopping at the place where the sentence first fails to make sense.

'She went to letter …'

This does not make sense.

2 Try replacing the word 'letter' with each of the remaining words in turn. Remember to ask yourself if the sentence makes sense each time.

  a 'She went to letter the write'   could become

       'She went to **the letter** write.'   **No**. This does not make sense.

  b 'She went to letter the write'   could become

       'She went to **write** the **letter**.'   **Yes**. The sentence now makes sense.

For the sentence to make sense, the words **letter** and **write** need to change places.

Selecting words

> **HAVE A GO**
>
> Find and underline the two words that need to change places to make a sensible sentence.
>
> a The kind dog adopted the stray lady.
>
> b How many divide can you times four into one hundred?
>
> c Last weekend, I went party my grandmother's birthday to.
>
> d What time does the start concert school this evening?

㉒ Rearrange words to find an unnecessary word

In this question type, you are asked to rearrange words into a sentence and find the word that is not required. A good understanding of how to structure a sensible sentence out of random words is key to solving these tricky questions.

Look at this example:

1 Scan the words quickly to try to understand the meaning of the sentence.

> Rearrange these words to make the longest sentence you can and underline the word that is not needed.
>
> sand   cat   across   endless   the   slithered   the   snake

2 Try to find two or more words that **logically** fit together and see if other words can be added to this word block:

  the endless sand (an expanse of sand is often referred to as endless)

  OR

  the snake slithered (this is how snakes move)

  OR

  slithered across (this is what a snake might do)

3 Place the blocks together to form a sentence, moving any words around until the sentence makes sense:

68 Selecting words

The snake slithered across the endless sand.

Don't worry if the sentence can be written in more than one way:

Across the endless sand, the snake slithered.

Sometimes the order of description can vary:

Across the endless sand, slithered the snake.

Remember, the question asks for the word that is not needed. The unnecessary word is **cat** because it does not fit anywhere in the sentence.

> **REMEMBER:** You don't have to write out the sentence in full. You just need to find the unnecessary word. However, it can be helpful to write out the sentence or to at least cross out or number the words as you go.

HAVE A GO

Rearrange the words to make the longest sentence you can and underline the word that is **not** needed.

a the puppy deserted the misty Rahul house from rescued.

b hot the plants leave the withered sun in.

c people decide the country are politicians of elected the by.

23 Select the best words to make a complete sentence

This question type tests your understanding of word definitions and how words relate to each other in sentences. You need to use this understanding to work out what would make sense within the **context** of a sentence.

Look at this example:

> Complete the following sentence by selecting the most sensible word from each group of words given in the brackets. Underline the words selected.
>
> The (children, books, foxes) carried the (houses, books, steps) home from the (cinema, library, factory).

Selecting words

Selecting words

The easiest way to solve questions like these is to break the sentence down into phrases. That way, you can assess what will be the most sensible answer for each section.

Section 1		Section 2		Section 3	
Options	Sensible?	Options	Sensible?	Options	Sensible?
The children carried	✓	carried the houses home	✗	books home from the cinema	✗
The books carried	✗	carried the books home	✓	books home from the library	✓
The foxes carried	unlikely	carried the steps home	unlikely	books home from the factory	unlikely

Putting the three most sensible options together, the answer is:

The (**children**, books, foxes) carried the (houses, **books**, steps) home from the (cinema, **library**, factory).

> **HAVE A GO**
>
> 1 Complete the following sentence by selecting the most sensible word from each group of words given in the brackets. Underline the words selected.
>
>   The recipe states that you need to (grow, bake, serenade) the cake in the (oven, shed, car) for two (weeks, years, hours).

Your understanding of word meanings, word **associations** and the use of context in a sentence is also tested in the following variation of this question type.

In these questions, one word in a given sentence must be replaced so that the sentence will make sense. You have to identify this word and think of a replacement word that will make the sentence sensible.

Look at this example:

> Change one word so that the sentence makes sense. Underline the word you are taking out and write your new word on the line.
>
> I waited in line to buy a book to see the film. _____

As with the previous question type, you can break the sentence down and look at it phrase by phrase. This will help you to check that each part links logically with the phrase before and after it.

I waited in line …	This phrase makes sense on its own.
… to buy a book …	This phrase makes sense on its own and when read with the first phrase.
… to see the film …	These words make sense on their own but not when read with the phrase before them. You don't buy a book to see a film.

What do you need to buy to see a film? A ticket. So underline the word **book** and write **ticket** on the line.

The sentence should be: I waited in line to buy a **ticket** to see the film.

HAVE A GO

2 Change one word so that the sentence makes sense. Underline the word you are taking out and write your new word on the line.

In winter, the average daily television is lower than it is in summer.

_____

The third version of this question type tests the same knowledge and skills as the previous two types, but this time you must also **evaluate** the options to select the **statement** that is always true.

Look at this example:

> Underline the word or phrase that makes this sentence true.
>
> A LIBRARY always has (posters, a carpet, books, DVDs, stairs).

It is likely that all the options given will make sense in the context of the statement. You must therefore check each word in turn and ask yourself a series of questions.

- Does a library always have posters?   NO, not always.   ✗
- Does a library always have a carpet?   Very likely, but NO, not always.   ✗
- Does a library always have books?   **YES**, always.   ✓
- Does a library always have DVDs?   Often, but NO, not always.   ✗
- Does a library always have stairs?   NO, not always.   ✗

Only one option is *always* true: A LIBRARY always has **books**.

HAVE A GO

3 Underline the word or phrase that makes this sentence true.

A FOREST always has (paths, birds, flowers, hedgehogs, trees).

24 Complete word analogies

These questions test your ability to spot a connection or relationship between two concepts or items and then apply the same link to something else. In verbal reasoning tests, word analogies can appear in several different forms. Let's look at them.

> **Complete the following expression by underlining the missing word.**
>
> **Pen is to ink as brush is to (sand, paper, paint).**

Here you are given one pair of words that are connected in a particular way. You are also given the first word of a second pair. You have to select the word that will complete the second pair in the same way as the first pair.

To do this, you need to work out the connection between the first pair.

So, in this example, you may think of the following relationship between 'pen' and 'ink':

　　　Pen is to ink – a pen makes a mark with ink

Now look at the first word of the second pair. Can you turn the connection you have found for the first pair into questions about the second pair?

Does a brush make a mark with sand?	No.
Does a brush make a mark with paper?	No.
Does a brush make a mark with paint?	**Yes**.

In this example, the word that will complete the second pair is **paint**.

> ### HAVE A GO
>
> **1** Complete the following expression by underlining the missing word.
>
> Pentagon is to five as heptagon is to (six, seven, eight).

This next version of a word **analogy** question also gives you a complete first pair and you must use your investigative skills to find the relationship between the words. The difference with this type of question is that you have to choose *both* words for the second pair from a set of options.

> Choose two words, one from each set of brackets, to complete the sentence in the best way.
>
> Smile is to happiness as (eat, tear, shout) is to (whisper, laugh, sorrow).

1 First, find the clear connection.

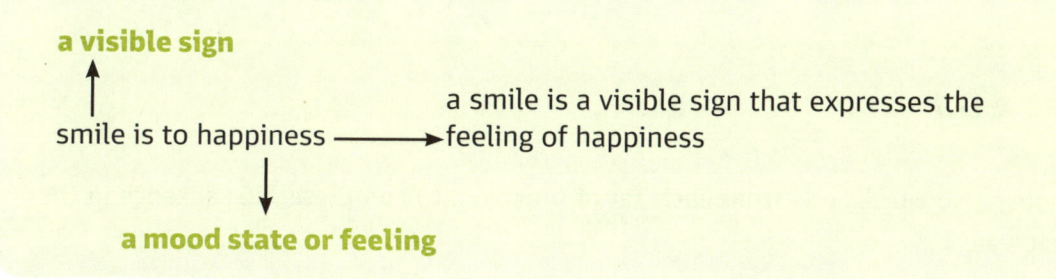

2 Take each word in the first set of brackets in turn. Look for the same connection with each word in the second set of brackets.

Selecting words

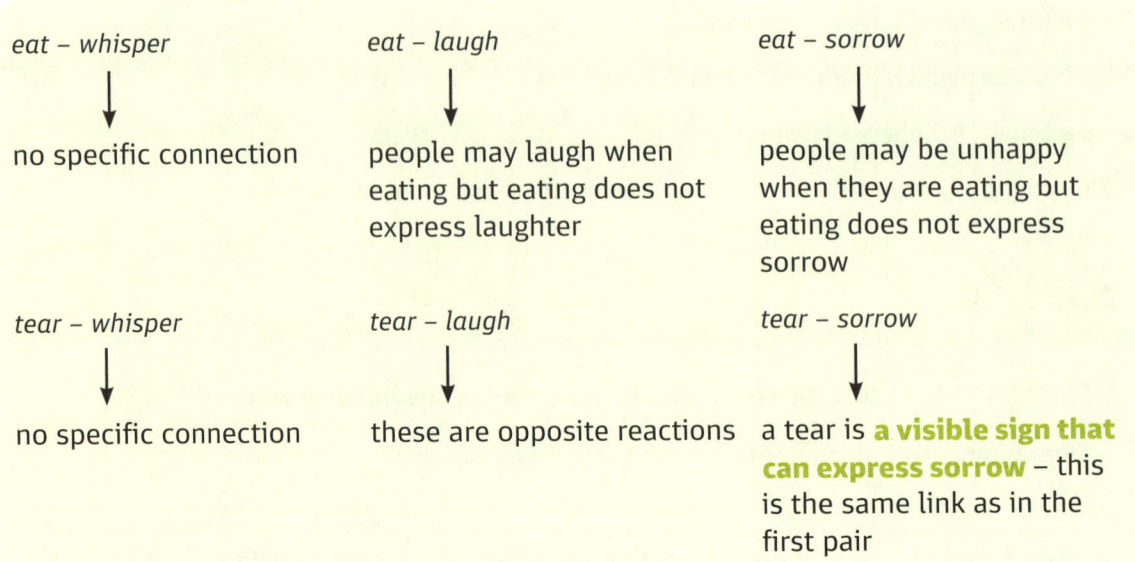

To make sure you have identified the correct pair of words, quickly work through the remaining options.

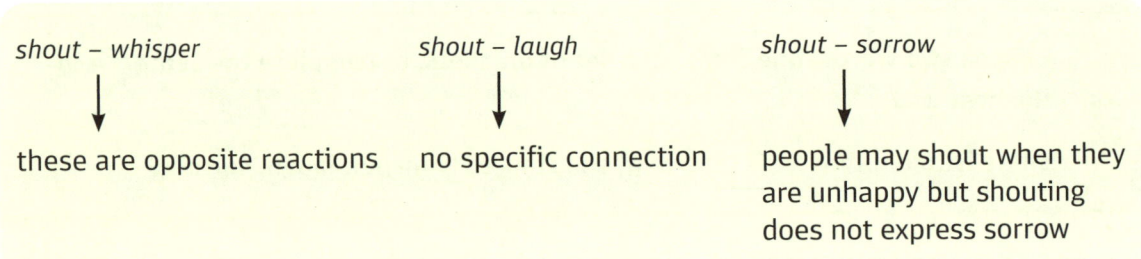

The answer to this example is therefore: Smile is to happiness **as tear is to sorrow**.

HAVE A GO

2 Choose two words, one from each set of brackets, to complete the sentence in the best way.

Swan is to cygnet as (goose, lion, cow) is to (foal, chick, gosling).

Not all analogies will show you the connection between the first pair of words. In this next variation, you need to find the same relationship for *both* pairs.

Look at this example:

> Complete the following sentence in the best way by choosing **one** word from each set of brackets.
>
> Tall is to (tree, short, colour) as narrow is to (thin, white, wide).

As before, work through each possible pair in the first set of brackets and try to find a clear connection that works in *both* parts of the sentence. Remember, the connection must be strong, not just a loose link with a topic or idea.

REMEMBER: It can sometimes seem that more than one answer is possible, but remember you are looking for the same link to complete both pairs.

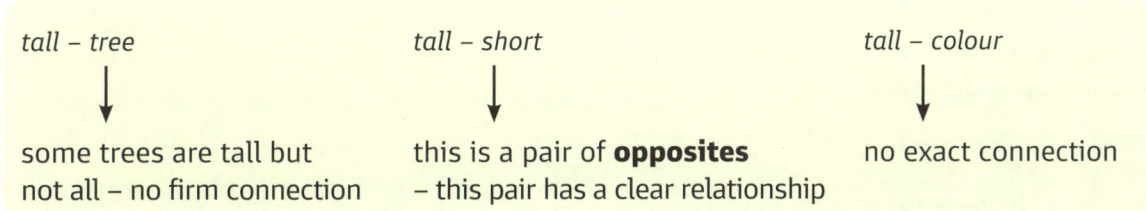

tall – tree	tall – short	tall – colour
some trees are tall but not all – no firm connection	this is a pair of **opposites** – this pair has a clear relationship	no exact connection

The most likely connection is that the pairs are opposites. Test this out on the second pair:

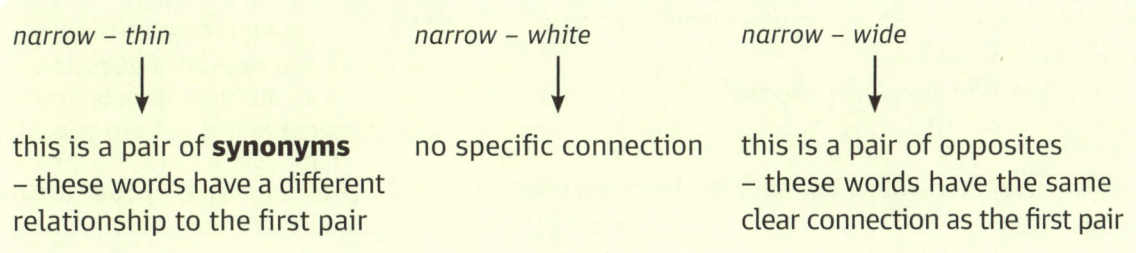

narrow – thin	narrow – white	narrow – wide
this is a pair of **synonyms** – these words have a different relationship to the first pair	no specific connection	this is a pair of opposites – these words have the same clear connection as the first pair

The words to select in this example are **short** and **wide**.

HAVE A GO

3 Complete the following sentence in the best way by choosing **one** word from each set of brackets.

a Gale is to (blow, wind, clouds) as blizzard is to (snow, cold, hurricane).

b Lively is to (hopeful, energetic, anxious) as sociable is to (healthy, friendly, moody).

Maths, sequences, coding and logic

There are nine types of verbal reasoning questions in this category:

- code using numbers, letters and symbols
- **logic** problems
- letter-coded sums
- complete the sum
- related numbers
- number sequences
- letter sequences
- letter analogies
- complete crosswords.

What skills do I need?

- sound mental arithmetic skills
- the ability to carry out calculations confidently using addition, subtraction, multiplication and division
- good knowledge of the times tables up to 12
- ability to follow sequences and identify patterns
- logic and **deduction**
- knowledge of alphabetical order.

As with most verbal reasoning question types, the key to tackling questions within this section is to work carefully and logically.

REMEMBER: With code and sequence questions, an alphabet line is often written out to help you. If it isn't, write out the alphabet on some spare paper before you start.

25 Code using numbers, letters and symbols

Several different variations of codes can appear in verbal reasoning papers. Code questions test your skills of deduction, your ability to find and use a given rule and your understanding of how words can be exchanged for letters, numbers or symbols.

This first question type uses symbols and you need to pay close attention to letter order to solve it.

Look at this example:

> If * £ / + is the code for READ, what is the code for ARE? Write the code on the line. _____

This is a straightforward code question type, as each symbol stands for a letter in the given word.

To make sure you match the right symbol to the right letter, write the symbols above the letters as shown here.

* £ / + ← code
R E A D ← given word

Now, look at the second word: ARE. All of the letters it is made up from appear in the first word. Match the letters to the correct symbol to encode each letter in turn. Remember to work through the letters in the word from left to right.

A becomes /
R becomes *
E becomes £

The code for A R E is **/ * £**.

HAVE A GO

1 If $ + * % ! is the code for SUITOR, what is the code for TOURS? Write the code on the line. _____

In the second variation of this question type, each word is given a number code and your task is to match each word to the correct number code.

Look at this example:

> The number codes for four words are listed in a random order.
>
> Find and underline the code for PAIL.
>
> 7133   3162   5462   5143
>
> PAIL   TALL   LANE   PINE

Maths, sequences, coding and logic

There are several ways of solving this question type as there are different letters you can start with, but they all follow the same thought process as shown in this example. Remember, these tests are timed so you need to find the fastest way to solve every question type!

First, look carefully at the four words given. What observations can you make?

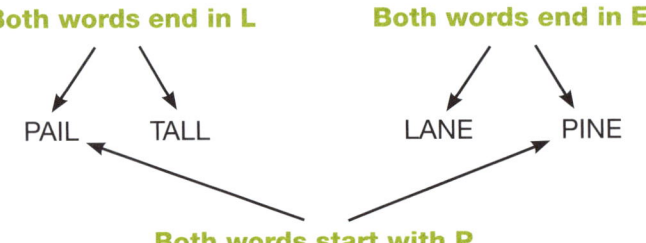

To find the answer as quickly as possible, you need to identify a feature that is unique to *one* of the words. Once you have done this, you can begin to **eliminate** the different options.

Only one word has a repeated letter.	TA**LL**
This means one of the codes will have a repeated number at the end.	71**33**
Therefore the code 7133 represents the word TALL.	T A L L
	7 1 3 3

From here, you can now answer the question, which is to find the code for PAIL. PAIL is the only other word that ends in the letter L, so its code must also end in the number 3.

The code must therefore be: P A I L

5 1 4 3

HAVE A GO

2 The number codes for four words are listed in a random order.

Find and underline the code for SALE.

9165	6185	2765	6512
PILE	LEAP	LACE	SALE

Other code questions use letters to form codes. This example is a similar question type to the code question using symbols we looked at earlier.

> If the code for ESCAPE is kdoryk, what is the code for PEAS? _____

You are given a word and its corresponding code. As for the symbols code question, start by writing the letters of the code above the word.

k d o r y k

E S C A P E

The word you have to encode is made up of letters found in the first word. Carefully matching the letters of the word to the correct code letter, work out the new code.

P	E	A	S
becomes	becomes	becomes	becomes
y	k	r	d

The code for PEAS is **ykrd**.

HAVE A GO

3 If the code for DELIGHT is xpbcswk, what is the code for GLIDE? _____

Some code questions are more complex and require you to be able to spot patterns as well as have a sound knowledge of alphabetical order.

Look at this example:

> If dkolepwh is the code for HOSPITAL what does the code xnawz stand for?
>
> _____

It is clear that the word you have to decode here includes different letters from those in the code for HOSPITAL.

Instead, you need to look at letter position in the alphabet to find the pattern or rule that has been applied.

Look again at the given word and its code:

d k o l e p w h

HOSPITAL

What connection can you find between each code letter and its corresponding word letter? Start by looking at the first few letters. Use an alphabet line to help you.

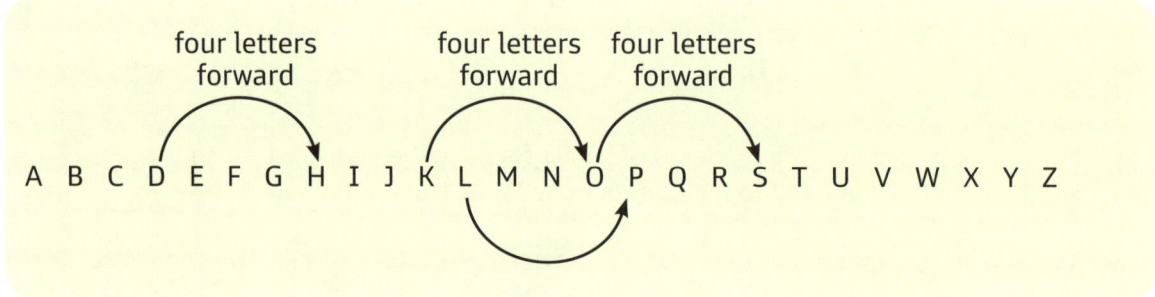

Is a pattern forming? Yes, it looks like each word letter is four places forward in the alphabet from its corresponding code letter. Check the remaining letters to confirm the pattern.

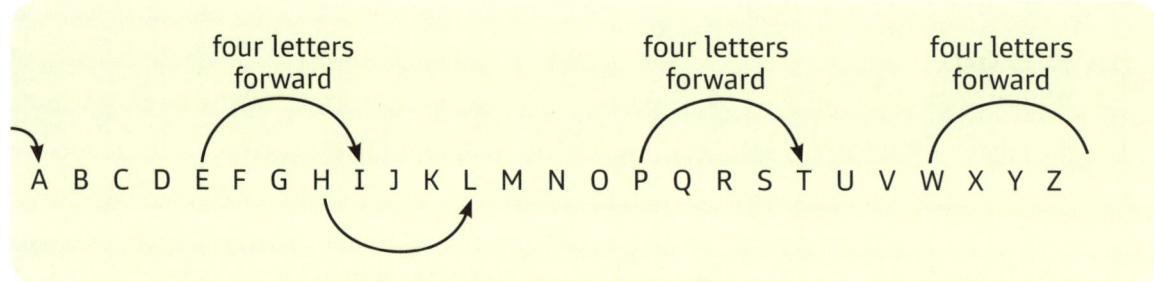

You can now apply this rule to the second coded word to find the answer.

x   four letters forward is   **B**

n   four letters forward is   **R**

a   four letters forward is   **E**   The answer is **bread**.

w   four letters forward is   **A**

z   four letters forward is   **D**

REMEMBER: Look out for alternate patterns!

HAVE A GO

4 Each question uses a different code. Use the alphabet to help you work out the answer to each question.

A B C D E F G H I J K L M N O P Q R S T U V W X Y Z

a If kvnqfs is the code for JUMPER, what does the code tdbsg stand for?

_____

b If the code for KNIGHT is lmjfis, what is the code for JOUST? _____

EXAM TIP

You need to work quickly in an exam to solve codes, so always look out for patterns. For example, in 'AZ, BY' there is a possible 'mirror image' pattern. If you are running out of time, check the first two codes and the last two codes to see if this shortcut reduces some of your options if you need to make an educated guess.

26 Logic problems

This question type relies on your ability to think logically. The questions test your skills of recognising key words and your ability to relate these facts to other clues. Sometimes, more than one answer may seem possible, but careful reading of all the clues available will help you eliminate the incorrect options.

Look at this example:

> Read the following statements and then underline the one of the four options below that must be true.
>
> 'Lions are animals. Animals are not stone.'
>
> A young lion's coat is spotty.
>
> Lions live in wildlife parks.
>
> Lions are not stone.
>
> Lions are animals because they hunt.

The first key point to draw out of the question is that it asks you to find the *one* **statement** that must be true. More than one of the statements may be true, but only one will be supported by the information given in the question.

REMEMBER: It often helps to 'read aloud' in your head when trying to concentrate on the meaning of sentences.

Working through a clear step-by-step process, like the one shown below, will help you eliminate the incorrect options.

1 Read each of the first two statements in turn, then think about two key questions:

What do they mean?

How do they relate to each other?

REMEMBER: Answer the question using just the information given, not your own opinion or general knowledge.

2 Now compare each of the options one by one with the first two statements. You may find it helpful to make notes in a table.
Lions are animals. Animals are not stone.

Option	Link with first statement?	Link with second statement?	Possible answer?
Young lions have spotty coats.	**Yes**, lions are mentioned in the first statement.	**No**, no mention of animals or stone.	✗
Lions live in wildlife parks.	**Yes**, lions are mentioned in the first statement.	**No**, no mention of animals or stone.	✗
Lions are not stone.	**Yes**, lions are mentioned in the first statement.	**Yes**, stone is mentioned in the second statement.	✓
Lions are animals because they hunt.	**Yes**, lions are mentioned in the first statement.	Animals are mentioned in the second statement but hunting is not.	✗

3 The correct option must have a strong link with both statements and only one possible answer has been identified in the table. Look at this option again to check how it relates to both statements.

Lions are not stone.	What are lions?	Lions are animals.
	Are animals stone?	No.
	How does this relate to both statements?	Lions are animals and, as animals are not stone, **lions are not stone**.

This option must be true according to the given information and is therefore the correct answer.

HAVE A GO

1 Read the following statements and then underline the one of the four options below that must be true.

Maisie must catch the bus at 8.00 a.m. to arrive at school on time. On Friday, Maisie caught the 8.20 a.m. bus.

Maisie got up late on Friday.

Maisie was absent from school on Friday.

Maisie likes school.

Maisie was late for school on Friday.

In the next variation, you are often given several statements to consider. You need to think about how each sentence relates to the information given in the rest of the statements. This type of question can often seem hard to solve. If you read each sentence carefully, and work out all of the information that can be gained from each one, you will find the correct answer.

Logic problems take a variety of forms and need to be tackled in different ways depending on the type of information given in the statements. The following three examples use different methods to find the answer.

The Browns live two houses away from the Wests.

The Wests are on the side of the road with even numbers and live at number 38.

The Wests are at the end of the road.

What is the house number of the Browns? _____

Once you have read through all of the statements carefully, take each sentence in turn and note down all of the information it gives. For this version of this question type, it can be helpful to note down the information in a diagram.

REMEMBER: Cross out each statement when you have taken all of the information from it.

1 The Browns live two houses away from the Wests.

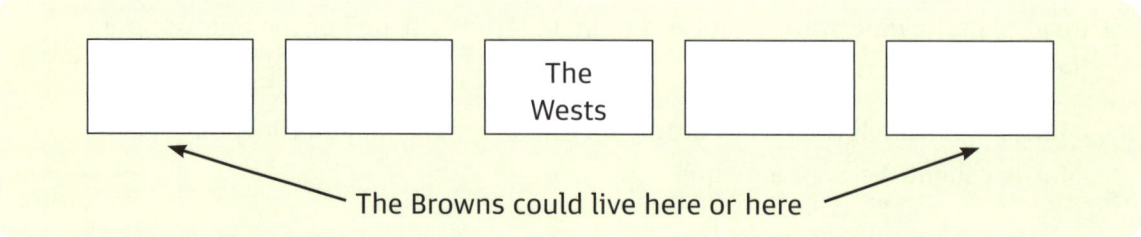

2 The Wests are on the side of the road with even numbers and they live at number 38.
   All houses must have even numbers; the numbers must go up or down by 2.

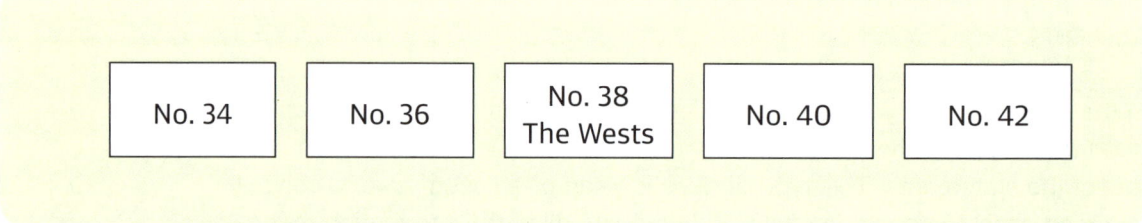

3 The Wests are at the end of the road.

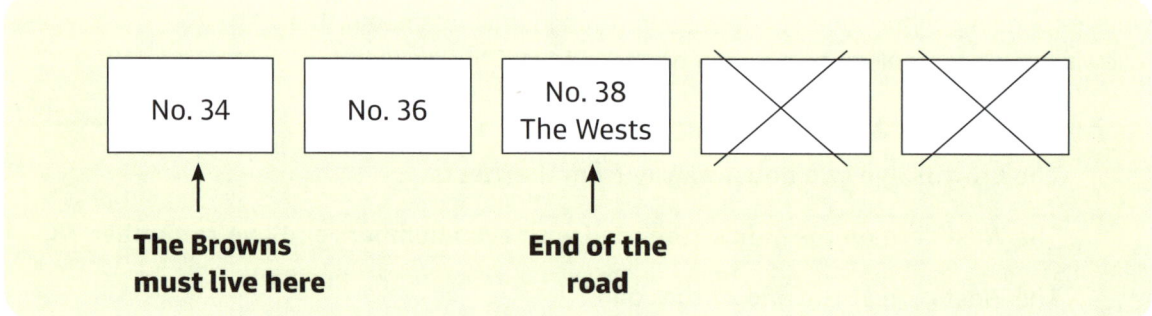

The Browns must live at house number **34**.

HAVE A GO

2 Five children are watching a pantomime at the theatre.

Jacob is sitting to Amiya's left. Clare and Amiya are going to share a bag of sweets so want to sit next to each other. Arjun chooses an end seat in case he needs to go to the toilet. Daisy is sitting to Clare's right. The children's teacher is sitting next to Daisy. The seat on the teacher's other side is empty.

Who is sitting next to Arjun? _____

Some logic problems are best solved by looking for a fact that is certain and then ordering the other information around it.

Look at this example:

> Seven horses are taking part in a race. Pepper is two places ahead of Willow. Scout is in first place and Rusty is two places behind him. Flash is currently in last place and is trying to overtake Nutmeg. Willow is three places ahead of Flash.
>
> In what place must Merlin be? _____

First, start by looking for the certain fact. In this question there are two facts that are certain: Scout is in first place and Flash is in last place.

The information can now be organised in a table with the places from first to last, starting with the two facts that you have been given.

Position	1st	2nd	3rd	4th	5th	6th	7th
Horse	Scout						Flash

Now it's time to sort out the rest of the information. If Rusty is two places behind Scout, that means Rusty is in 3rd place. Willow is three places ahead of Flash, making her in 4th place. Pepper is two places ahead of Willow, putting him in 2nd place. Flash is trying to overtake Nutmeg, which means Nutmeg is placed 6th.

Your table now looks like this.

Position	1st	2nd	3rd	4th	5th	6th	7th
Horse	Scout	Pepper	Rusty	Willow		Nutmeg	Flash

By ordering the information, it is now clear that Merlin must be in **5th** place.

HAVE A GO

3 Five children were comparing scores in last week's spelling challenge. Out of 100 questions, Jamie got half of them correct. Saira came second, scoring just six marks less than the winning result and twenty more than Will, who scored 64. The highest score belonged to Zak, who got twice as many questions correct as Megan.

Which child finished in 3rd place? _____

In this final example, you will see that organising all of the information in a grid is the most helpful method for solving this type of problem.

Adam, Daniel, Matthew, Ranjana and Sarah are 10, 9, 8, 7 and 6 years old but not in that order. Sarah is older than Ranjana. Adam is older than Daniel. Matthew is two years younger than Ranjana. Daniel is two years younger than Matthew.

Who is the youngest? _____

Draw a grid showing the names of the children and the age range.

Now think about each statement in turn. What information does each one give you? As you work out what information each statement holds, mark off the appropriate boxes in the grid.

REMEMBER: You need to extract the maximum amount of information from each statement before moving on.

Sarah is older than Ranjana, so:

- Sarah cannot be 6.
- Ranjana cannot be 10.
- The youngest cannot be Sarah.

	Sarah	Ranjana	Adam	Daniel	Matthew
Age 10		✗			
Age 9					
Age 8					
Age 7					
Age 6	✗				

Adam is older than Daniel, so:

- Adam cannot be 6.
- Daniel cannot be 10.
- The youngest cannot be Adam.

	Sarah	Ranjana	Adam	Daniel	Matthew
Age 10		✗		✗	
Age 9					
Age 8					
Age 7					
Age 6	✗		✗		

Matthew is two years younger than Ranjana, so:

- Matthew cannot be 9 or 10.
- Ranjana cannot be 6 or 7.
- Ranjana cannot be the youngest.

	Sarah	Ranjana	Adam	Daniel	Matthew
Age 10		✗		✗	✗
Age 9					✗
Age 8					
Age 7		✗			
Age 6	✗	✗	✗		

Daniel is two years younger than Matthew, so:

- Matthew cannot be 6 or 7.
- Daniel cannot be 9 or 10.
- Matthew cannot be the youngest.

	Sarah	Ranjana	Adam	Daniel	Matthew
Age 10		✗		✗	✗
Age 9					✗
Age 8					
Age 7		✗			✗
Age 6	✗	✗	✗		✗

We now know that **Daniel** must be the youngest as he is the only child who doesn't have a ✗ in the Age 6 row.

REMEMBER: Don't become distracted trying to fill the grid in completely. You only need to find the answer to the question!

HAVE A GO

4 Sophie, Carlos, Sunita, Amir and Leah are talking about the leisure activities they do at the weekend. Sophie and Amir both swim on Saturday morning, while Carlos and Leah enjoy going ice-skating. Sunday morning football training is enjoyed by Sunita and Carlos, while Sophie and Leah go to a local drama club. Amir catches up on homework on Sunday morning, but in the afternoon, he usually joins Carlos at the leisure centre for tennis training. All the children except Sophie attend the free Saturday afternoon roller disco.

Who does the most activities? _____

27 Letter-coded sums

This question type tests your **number bonds** knowledge, but you also need to understand how simple **substitutions** work, interchanging numbers and letters. Your ability to think logically and work carefully is also important.

Look at this example:

> If A = 1, B = 2, C = 3, D = 4 and E = 5:
>
> **a** Find the sum of this word: BEAD _____
>
> **b** Give the answer to this calculation as a letter.   B + D − E = _____

To answer part **a**:

1 First, make sure you understand what the question is asking you to do. Find the sum means 'find the total **value** by adding together'.
2 Next, match each letter with its corresponding number value.
3 Now, add together all of the numbers to find the answer.
   2 + 5 + 1 + 4 = 12

B	E	A	D
2	5	1	4

The value of the word BEAD is **12**.

To answer part **b**, you need to find the answer to the given **equation**. In order to do this, you must change the format of the equation.

REMEMBER: Be careful to answer all parts of a question if it has multiple parts.

1 Match each letter with its corresponding number value.

B	D	E
2	4	5

2 Rewrite the equation, exchanging the letters for numbers. Make sure you keep the right signs.

B + D − E =

2 + 4 − 5 =

3 Solve the calculation.

2 + 4 − 5 = 1

4 Check which letter has the corresponding value and write in the answer.

1 = **A**

REMEMBER: Check how you need to write the answer. If you leave the answer as a number when the question has asked for it to be written as a letter, it will be marked as incorrect!

The answer to this example is **A**.

HAVE A GO

If B = 3, C = 5, I = 7, K = 9 and R = 11:

a Find the sum of this word: BRICK _____

b Give the answer to this calculation as a letter. R − C + B = _____

c Give the answer to this calculation as a number. K × R = _____

d Give the answer to this calculation as a number. (K ÷ B) × C = _____

EXAM TIP

If no signs and no instructions are given for a calculation, assume that the letters of a word are added together. This is different from maths where, in algebra, letters next to each other with no sign in between are multiplied.

28 Complete the sum

This question type tests your ability to use **inverse operations** to make a sum balance. Being able to switch quickly and confidently between addition and subtraction, and multiplication and division will help you to solve these questions.

Look at this example:

> Find the missing number to complete the sum. Write your answer on the line.
>
> 10 ÷ 2 = 3 + _____

The sum needs to balance on either side of the equals sign. Start by working out the answer to the sum on the left of the equals sign and write the answer to this part of the sum above it like this:

    5
10 ÷ 2 = 3 + _____

Maths, sequences, coding and logic

Now you can find out what the missing number is by doing an *inverse* operation with the numbers you have been given. Take the 3 over to the left side of the equals sign and subtract it from 5 like this:

$$5 - 3 = 2$$

So the missing number is **2** and the completed sum now looks like this:

$$5 = 5$$

$$10 \div 2 = 3 + \mathbf{2}$$

HAVE A GO

Find the missing number to complete each sum. Write the number on the line.

a $24 \div 8 = 9 - $ _____

b $8 \times 7 = 45 + $ _____

c $21 - 15 = 72 \div $ _____

d $16 \div 2 + 7 = 3 + 17 - $ _____

e $7 \times 6 - 10 = 8 \times $ _____

㉙ Related numbers

In this question type, your task is to discover the rule or connection between the numbers in the first two sets and then apply the same rule to the third set of numbers.

Look at this example:

> Find the number that completes the final set of numbers in the same way as the first two sets. Write the number on the line.
>
> 4 [32] 8   6 [42] 7   8 [_____] 9

To solve the question, start by looking for a relationship between the numbers in the first set.

The number inside the brackets has been made in some way from the two numbers either side.

To find the answer, consider each of the four mathematical operations in turn (+ − × ÷).

As the number in the brackets is larger than both of the numbers either side, it makes sense to start with the operations that make numbers larger, which are addition and multiplication. So start by adding the first and third numbers together:

4 + 8 = 12

This isn't the answer we are looking for, so now move on to trying multiplication.

4 × 8 = 32

This has produced the correct answer, so the rule may be to multiply the outer numbers, but you need to check that the same process also works for the middle set of numbers before applying it to the third set, as it MUST work for all three sets.

6 × 7 = 42

We have proved that the rule works for both sets, so we can now go ahead and apply it to complete the last set.

8 × 9 = ?

The answer is 72, so the missing middle number is **72**.

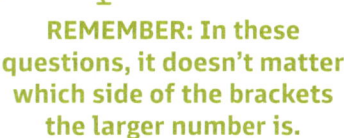

REMEMBER: In these questions, it doesn't matter which side of the brackets the larger number is.

HAVE A GO

1 Find the number that completes the final set of numbers in the same way as the first two sets. Write the number on the line.

16 [25] 9   7 [20] 13   14 [_____] 12

In the next example, the number in the brackets is smaller than the number on the left, so we need to use an operation that will *decrease* the numbers. Our options this time are *subtraction* and *division*.

Find the number that completes the final set of numbers in the same way as the first two sets. Write the number on the line.

56 [8] 7   70 [7] 10   54 [_____] 6

Let's try subtraction first.

$56 - 7 = 49$

This isn't the answer we're looking for, so move on to division.

$56 \div 7 = 8$

This is the correct answer, so we may have found the rule, but remember to check it works with the middle set before applying it to the final set.

$70 \div 10 = 7$

The rule works for both sets, so we can now use it to work out the missing number in the third set.

$54 \div 6 = 9$

Therefore, the missing number is **9**.

> ### HAVE A GO
>
> 2 Find the number that completes the final set of numbers in the same way as the first two sets. Write the number on the line.
>
>   72 [8] 9   49 [7] 7   108 [_____] 12

Sometimes it is necessary to perform more than one calculation to find the correct answer.

Look at this example:

> **Find the number that completes the final set of numbers in the same way as the first two sets.**
>
> 3 [7] 11   15 [18] 21   14 [_____] 26

If you try using a one-step calculation with any of the four operations (+ − × ÷), you will find that it doesn't work for this question. We need to do a second calculation to find the answer.

Set 1

3 [7] 11

Start with addition.

Step 1: 3 + 11 = 14

The answer is greater than 7, in fact it is *double* the number we are looking for. So we can *halve* it to get the answer we need.

Step 2: 14 ÷ 2 = 7

Let's check that the rule works for the middle set.

Set 2

15 [18] 21

Step 1: 15 + 21 = 36

Step 2: 36 ÷ 2 = 18

It works, so now you can move on to working out the missing number in the third set.

Set 3

14 [_____] 26

Step 1: 14 + 26 = 40

Step 2: 40 ÷ 2 = 20

So, the missing number is **20**.

HAVE A GO

3 Find the number that completes the final set of numbers in the same way as the first two sets. Write the number on the line.

4 [20] 6   6 [16] 2   11 [_____] 1

This question type can be further extended by number problems that involve using an extra number.

Look at this example:

> Find the number that completes the final set of numbers in the same way as the first two sets.
>
> 12 [4] 4   18 [7] 3   24 [_____] 6

The middle numbers in the first two sets are smaller than the larger of the two numbers outside the brackets, indicating that a maths process that reduces the value will probably be required. So we need to look at subtraction and division.

Let's try subtraction first.

Set 1

12 [4] 4

Step 1: 12 − 4 = 8

In order to get to the answer of 4, we need to reduce the total further by either dividing by 2 or subtracting 4.

Step 2: 8 ÷ 2 = 4 or 8 − 4 = 4

Does this process work with the second set of numbers?

Set 2

18 [7] 3

Step 1: 18 − 3 = 15

Step 2: 15 ÷ 2 − 7.5 ✗   15 − 4 = 11 ✗

This method doesn't work for the second set; therefore, it is not the right method.

Now let's try division.

Set 1

12 [4] 4

Step 1: 12 ÷ 4 = 3

To get to the answer of 4, we can add an extra 1.

Step 2: 3 + 1 = 4

Check that the method works with the second set.

Set 2

18 [7] 3

Step 1: 18 ÷ 3 = 6

Step 2: 6 + 1 = 7

As this method works for both sets, it is the correct method and can be applied to the third set of numbers.

Set 3

24 [_____] 6

Step 1: 24 ÷ 6 = 4

Step 2: 4 + 1 = 5

The correct answer is therefore **5**.

For questions like the example above, the extra number is usually quite small and may be added or subtracted.

> **HAVE A GO**
>
> **4** Find the number that completes the final set of numbers in the same way as the first two sets. Write the number on the line.
>
> 13 [2] 9   7 [1] 4   11 [_____] 6

30 Number sequences

Number sequences test your ability to work out a rule and then apply it correctly to complete the sequence. You will also need to be able to confidently use the four number operations (addition, subtraction, multiplication and division) to find the patterns in number sequences.

Look at this example:

> Give the two missing numbers in the following sequence. Write the numbers on the lines.
>
> 2   4   6   8   _____   _____

You may be able to see a pattern straight away, but don't worry if you can't.

Working from left to right, look at the numbers in pairs and note down the difference from one number to the next.

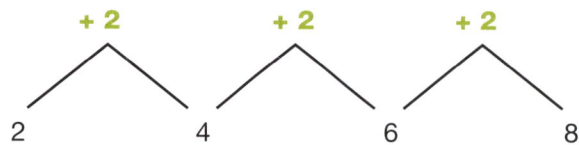

This shows a clear regular pattern: the numbers increase by 2 each time.

You can now apply this rule to the next two numbers and complete the sequence.

HAVE A GO

1 Give the two missing numbers in the following sequences. Write the numbers on the lines.

   a 3   6   12   24   _____ _____

   b 2   5   9   14   _____ _____

   c 64   56   48   40   _____ _____

Not all number sequences will use regular patterns (such as + 1, + 2 or – 2, – 2) each time. Some patterns may go alternately in pairs. If the numbers are not *all* getting bigger or smaller, but appear to move around randomly, there may be *two* **alternating sequences** going on.

Look at the next example.

> Give the two missing numbers in the following sequence. Write the numbers on the lines.
>
> 5   21   8   17   11   13   _____ _____

First, check the difference between each pair of numbers as before.

There is no clear or regular pattern between the numbers. Instead, try looking at every other number.

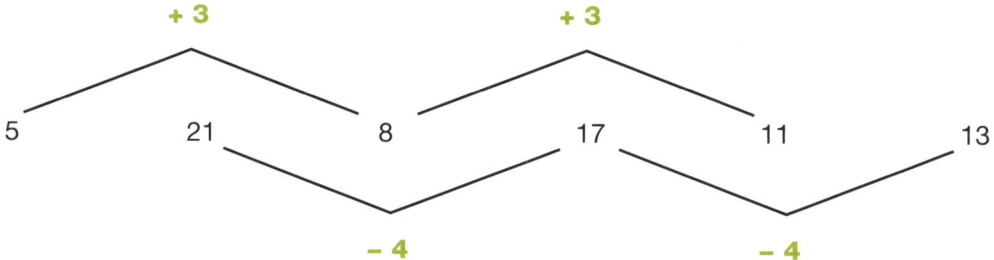

By looking at the difference between alternate numbers, we can identify two clear patterns:

- the first, third and fifth numbers *increase* by 3 each time
- the second, fourth and sixth numbers *decrease* by 4 each time.

You can now apply these rules to the next two numbers in the sequence. Make sure you use the right rule with the right number!

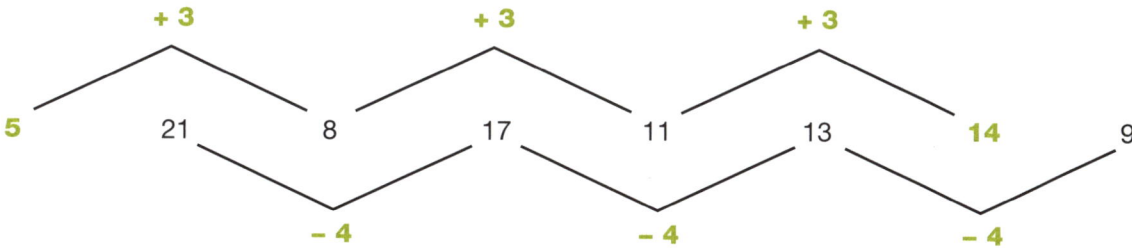

HAVE A GO

2 Give the two missing numbers in the following sequences. Write the numbers on the lines.

a 6   20   8   15   10   10   ____ ____

b 9   7   13   6   17   5   ____ ____

c 16   16   13   8   10   4   ____ ____

31 Letter sequences

Letter sequences follow the same principle as number sequences, in that there is a rule or pattern that you need to discover and then apply it correctly in order to be able to work out the next pair of letters.

Look at this example:

> Give the missing pair of letters in the following sequence. The alphabet has been written out to help you. Write the next pair of letters on the line.
>
> A B C D E F G H I J K L M N O P Q R S T U V W X Y Z
>
> A B   E F   I J   M N   _____

Working carefully from left to right, we can see that each pair of letters consists of letters that follow **consecutively** in the alphabet. Between each pair of letters there is a gap of two letters. Therefore the next pair of letters that follows MN is **QR**.

HAVE A GO

1 Give the missing pair of letters in the following sequence. The alphabet has been written out to help you. Write the next pair of letters on the line.

A B C D E F G H I J K L M N O P Q R S T U V W X Y Z

Z Y   Y X   X W   W V   _____

Here is another more challenging example.

> Give the two missing pairs of letters in the following sequence. The alphabet has been written out to help you. Write the letter pairs on the lines.
>
> A B C D E F G H I J K L M N O P Q R S T U V W X Y Z
>
> C Q   D Q   E P   F P   _____   _____

If you look at each pair of letters individually, following the same process as before, you will find that there is no clear pattern between the letters.

To solve this question, you need to look at the *first* letters of each pair together and then the *second* letters of each pair together.

Sequence of the **first** letters: **C, D, E, F**

A B **C D E F** G ...

These are consecutive letters.

Sequence of the **second** letters: **Q, Q, P, P**

The second letter of the first and second pairs is Q.

N O **P Q** R S T ...

The second letter of the third and fourth pairs is P. These are consecutive letters but they are going backwards.

A clear pattern has been identified and the rules can now be applied to complete the sequence.

The first letters of the next two pairs will be: **G H**

The second letters of the next two pairs will be: **O O**

So the completed sequence will read: C Q   D Q   E P   F P   **G O**   **H O**

HAVE A GO

2 Give the two missing pairs of letters in the following sequence. The alphabet has been written out to help you. Write the letters on the lines.

A B C D E F G H I J K L M N O P Q R S T U V W X Y Z

A Z   B Y   D W   G T   _____   _____

Not all letter sequences will use regular patterns. Some patterns may go *alternately*.

Maths, sequences, coding and logic 99

Look at this example:

> **Give the two missing pairs of letters in the following sequence. The alphabet has been written out to help you. Write the letter pairs on the lines.**
>
> A B C D E F G H I J K L M N O P Q R S T U V W X Y Z
>
> D E   Z Y   F G   X W   H I   V U   ___   ___

Alternating sequences can be solved by following the letters consecutively, but they rely on very careful counting as there are big gaps between the letters and it can be difficult to detect a clear pattern. A more effective strategy for solving this type of question is to look at every alternate pair of letters.

Starting with the sequence beginning D E, we can count two letters forward from D E to F G and two again from G F to H I. The rule is + 2 letters. The next pair of letters will therefore be **J K**.

D E   Z Y   F G   X W   H I   V U   ___   ___

Now look at the second sequence starting ZY.

D E   Z Y   F G   X W   H I   V U   ___   ___

Z Y to X W is two letters backwards and X W to V U is the same. The rule is therefore − 2 letters. Using this rule, we can work out that the next pair of letters will be **T S**.

Don't forget that if the sequence goes further than the end of the alphabet, either forwards or backwards, imagine the alphabet running in a circle and continue back round to the beginning of the alphabet.

HAVE A GO

3 Give the two missing pairs of letters in the following sequence. The alphabet has been written out to help you. Write the letters on the lines.

A B C D E F G H I J K L M N O P Q R S T U V W X Y Z

Q R   G F   S T   E D   U V   C B   ___   ___

Maths, sequences, coding and logic

32 Letter analogies

The first question type is a form of **analogy** (see also 26 Complete word analogies) where you have to spot the connection between pairs of letters and apply the rule to the missing letters.

Look at this example:

> Fill in the missing letters. The alphabet has been written out to help you. Write the answer on the line.
>
> A B C D E F G H I J K L M N O P Q R S T U V W X Y Z
>
> A B is to C D as P Q is to _____

Start by looking at the first pair of letters and then the second pair. What do you notice? Use the alphabet line to help you.

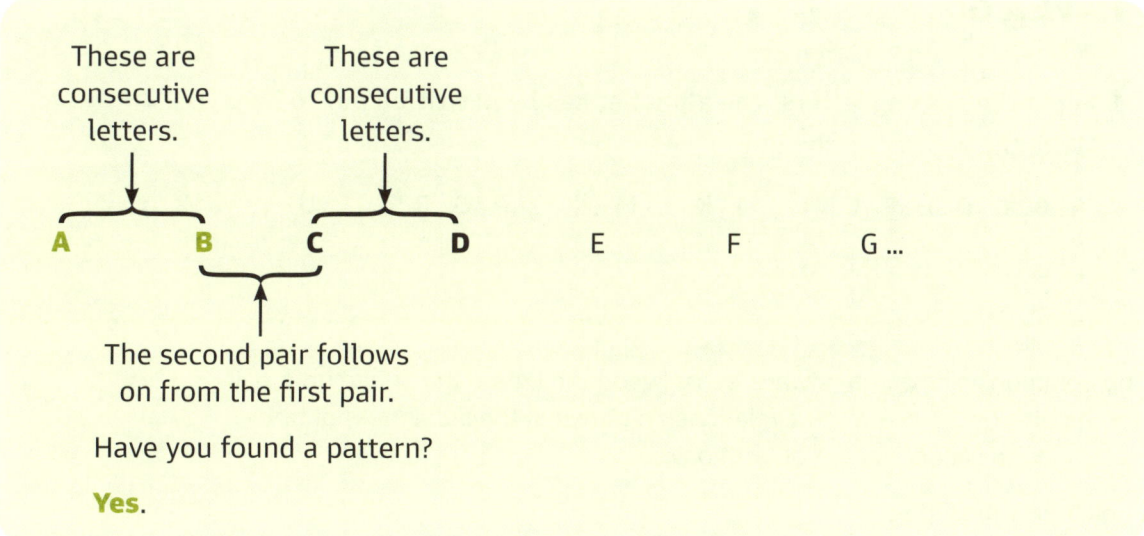

Have you found a pattern?

Yes.

The first and second pairs are made up of consecutive letters and the second pair follows on from the first pair. Does the third pair follow the first part of this pattern?

K L M N O **P Q** ...

Apply the rule to the missing letters to complete the analogy.

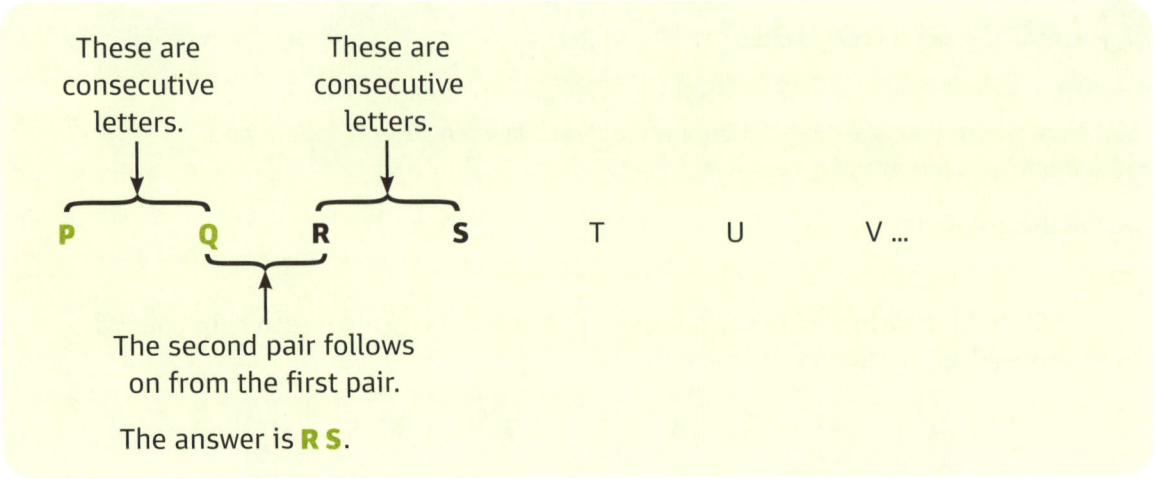

In the example above, the third pair of letters follows on consecutively from the second pair, but it is important to remember that this is *not* always the case.

HAVE A GO

1 Fill in the missing letters. The alphabet has been written out to help you. Write the answer on the line.

A B C D E F G H I J K L M N O P Q R S T U V W X Y Z

J I is to H G as S R is to _____

The common link may not always be *between* the letters that make up a pair. Some patterns are based on a relationship between the *first* letters of both pairs and the *second* letters of both pairs.

Look at this example:

Fill in the missing letters. The alphabet has been written out to help you. Write the answer on the line.

A B C D E F G H I J K L M N O P Q R S T U V W X Y Z

G X is to J U as S F is to _____

Here we have to look at the first letters of each pair to understand the relationship.

G is to J

We have to count how many letters are between G and J and check whether we are moving forwards through the alphabet or backwards.

To get from G to J we move *forwards* three letters.

Now we need to check the relationship between the second letters of each pair to see if it is the same or something different.

X is to U

Count how many letters there are between X and U. There are three letters between them and we are moving *backwards* through the alphabet.

It can be helpful to show your working like this:

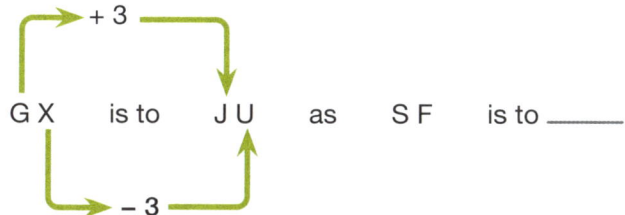

Now you can apply the same rule to the pair of letters you have been given to work with.

S F is to ? ?

Start with the first letter, S and count three letters forward, which gives us V.

Now move on to the second letter of the pair, F, and count three letters backwards, which gives us C.

So the answer is **V C**.

HAVE A GO

2 Fill in the missing letters. The alphabet has been written out to help you. Write the answer on the line.

A B C D E F G H I J K L M N O P Q R S T U V W X Y Z

X C is to T E as W B is to _____

Maths, sequences, coding and logic

More challenging questions of this type require you to imagine the alphabet as a circle, with A and Z next to each other.

Look at this example:

> **Fill in the missing letters. The alphabet has been written out to help you. Write the answer on the line.**
>
> A B C D E F G H I J K L M N O P Q R S T U V W X Y Z
>
> B K is to W O as J Y is to _____

Starting with the first letter of each pair, we have to count the letters to get from B to W. It would take too long to count forwards so the quickest way is to go backwards.

Imagining the alphabet as a circle, we can count five letters *backwards* to get from B to W.

Let's look at the second letters. To get from K to O, count *forwards* four letters.

Now we know what the rule is, we can find the solution to the third pair of letters, J A.

Counting five steps backwards from J gives us E and four steps forward from X is B. So the answer is **E B**.

HAVE A GO

3 Fill in the missing letters. The alphabet has been written out to help you. Write the answer on the line.

A B C D E F G H I J K L M N O P Q R S T U V W X Y Z

E O is to Z S as L X is to _____

Another variation of this question type uses a mixture of letters and numbers.

Look at this example:

> **Fill in the missing letters and numbers. The alphabet has been written out to help you. Write the answer on the line.**
>
> A B C D E F G H I J K L M N O P Q R S T U V W X Y Z
>
> D 3 is to H 6 as N 9 is to _____

Let's start by looking at the letters.

Counting from D to H is four letters forward, so we can do the same with N to get the letter R.

Now look at the numbers.

The first number is 3 and the next one is 6, so that is a gap of three. Following this rule we can count three more from 9, which gives the answer of 12.

So the correct answer to the question is **R 12**.

> **REMEMBER:** A common pitfall with this question type is to confuse letter pairs with letter sequences. In letter pairs and letter/number pairs, there is no link between the second and third pairs, so remember not to count between them.

HAVE A GO

4 Fill in the missing letters and numbers. The alphabet has been written out to help you. Write the answer on the line.

A B C D E F G H I J K L M N O P Q R S T U V W X Y Z

Z 5 is to U 10 as C 2 is to _____

33 Complete crosswords

Spelling, logical thinking and awareness of letter position within words are all skills that will help with crossword reasoning questions.

Look at this example:

> **Fill in the crossword so that all the given words are included. You have been given one letter as a clue.**
>
> *patent, feeler,*
> *atoned, fasten,*
> *stolen, snored*

Maths, sequences, coding and logic

1 Use the given clue to get started.

Which word (or words) has 'S' as a third letter? FASTEN

Any others?   No.

So the word **FASTEN** can be put in.

This will now give the second letter for each of the words going down.

2 Work your way along the letters, starting with the first column.

Which of the remaining words has 'A' as a second letter? PATENT

Any others?   No.

PATENT can be written in the grid.

3 Following this process, you will find that there are two words that could fit in the second column – ATONED and STOLEN – as they both have 'T' as a second letter. Move on to the next column and come back to these options once you have put the other words in the grid.

4 Look at the final column.

Which of the remaining words has 'N' as a second letter? SNORED

Any others? No.

SNORED can be written in the grid.

5 Now consider the words going across.

Which of the remaining words has 'E' as a second letter? FEELER

Any others? No.

FEELER can be written in the grid.

6 The two remaining words are ATONED and STOLEN. It is now clear where these two words go and the crossword can be completed:

> **REMEMBER:** You may find it useful to cross through each of the options as you write them into the grid.

HAVE A GO

Fill in the crossword so that all the given words are included.
You have been given one letter as a clue.

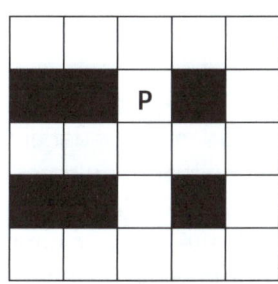

a apple, paper, years, syrup, sheep

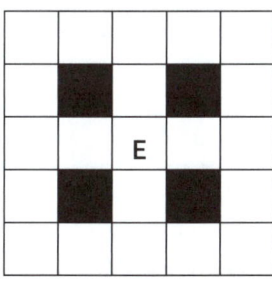

b heron, meter, reels, their, risen, marsh

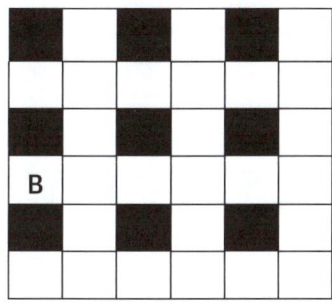

c bedsit, comets, absorb, obtuse, abrupt, bureau

Skills builder

Try some of these activities to help improve your verbal reasoning 11+ skills, some at home, some out and about.

VERBAL REASONING AT HOME

- Try fun board games that improve spelling and vocabulary such as Scrabble, Bananagrams, Articulate, Boggle, Codenames, and Scattergories.

- Often libraries have games to borrow, and charity shops are great places to buy them too. Try Dabble, Guess Who?, Tension and Risk to help with your logical thinking and problem-solving skills.

- Chill out with some music and the *Bond Brain Training Logic Book* and *Bond Brain Training Word Book*.

- Make word searches for your friends. Research topics that interest you and construct a puzzle based on them.

- For exposure to a wide range of general knowledge, try games like Trivial Pursuit, The Chase, Mapominoes and Globe Runner.

- If you want to wind down with a game on your computer, console, or tablet, go for Big Brain Academy, Solitaire or The Sims.

- Crossword books for children can often be bought cheaply online and from newsagents. These are great for extending your vocabulary and are satisfying to complete too!

Skills builder

OUT AND ABOUT VERBAL REASONING

- Play Conundrum with family and friends. One person thinks of a word, makes an anagram of it and the other person has to guess the word from the anagram. You can give clues like, 'This word is a synonym for weak.'

- If you have a paper and pencil or a phone with a notes app, you can play Constantinople. A parent or friend challenges you with a long word (8+ letters) and you have to rearrange the letters to find as many smaller words within it as possible.

- Great pen and paper games include Battleships, Noughts and Crosses, Connect Four, and Dots and Boxes.

- Word links: The first person says a word and the next person finds another word that links to this first word. For example, 'learning', 'school' (you learn at school), 'dolphin' (dolphins live in schools), 'elephant' (dolphins and elephants are both mammals).

- Use the time you are travelling, walking or waiting to play games like Word links, Who Am I?, and Alphabet categories.

- Word chains: Start with a four- or five-letter word, then change just one letter at a time, seeing how long a chain of different words you can make. For example: *read*, *real*, *heal*, *hell*, *held*, *hold*, *sold*.

- Who am I?: Guess who someone is thinking of by using yes/no questions. For example, 'Are you fictional?' (Yes.); 'Are you a cartoon character?' (No.); 'Are you on television?' (Yes,); 'Are you an animal?' (No.); 'Are you a human?' (No.); 'Are you an alien?' (Yes.); 'Do you travel in space and time?' (Yes); Are you The Doctor? (YES!)

- Run around synonyms and antonyms: In an outdoor space, choose a place that is designated 'Synonyms' and one that is designated 'Antonyms'. Ask your parent/guardian to say a word and then give either a synonym or an antonym. Run to the correct place. This is a fun game to play in competition with friends.

- Ball bounce spelling: Ask a parent/guardian or friend to give you a word to spell. Then, bounce a ball to each other, one bounce for each letter of the spelling. If the ball goes out of control or if the spelling is incorrect, the next player takes the ball. Try and bounce and spell as quickly as you can.

- Alphabet categories: Choose a theme (for example, names, food items, places, television characters). The first person says a word that fits the theme and that begins with A. The next person finds a word beginning with B. Keeping going until you reach Z.

- Ball throw words: Stand in a circle with friends. Choose a topic like 'Food beginning with A'. Throw the ball randomly around the circle, giving a correct word each time.

- There are plenty of games that are more active and involve groups of children or family members.

Skills builder

LEARNING AND PRACTISING VERBAL REASONING SKILLS

- Build up knowledge of words that have common links by naming five or ten types of food/buildings/vehicles and so on in one minute. No exam will include top tracks by your favourite artist or top footballers from your favourite team, but this will help you to think quickly and accurately.

- Take a song or poem and change as many of the words or phrases as possible into synonyms. For example, 'Twinkle, twinkle little star, how I wonder what you are' could become: 'Glistening, shimmering tiny star, how I marvel at what you are.'

- Ask a parent/guardian to give you a group of words and try to guess the link between them. For example, pencil, pen, chalk are all writing implements; torch, lamp, candle are all sources of light.

- Keep a tally of all the compound words you use during the day. Whether it is going 'upstairs' to your 'bedroom', going 'outside' to build a 'snowman' or to play 'football', try actively looking for compound words.

- Do a sort out. Clear out a drawer or cupboard and group items logically. Devise a plan for where they should go and your reasons why.

- Create a code to communicate with your friends. Letters can be transposed + 1 or − 1, so 'Hello' becomes 'Ifmmp' or 'Gdkkn'.

- In the supermarket or food shops, make a point of picking out the different items of food in categories, for example: 'We need some dairy items, so what is here that is a dairy item?' Try to list as many dairy items as you can see.

- Once a day, impress your friends and family by describing something in the most exaggerated way possible, using a wide range of descriptive words. For example, a school blazer might be described as, 'A delightful hue of midnight blue with a delicate band of shimmering, iridescent azure that frames the superbly designed pockets in the most spectacular way possible.' Use a thesaurus to find as many new descriptive words as you can.

Study guide

You've worked through this book. Now test yourself!

1. Build confidence with practice

For more practice, and to put your skills to the test, work through the range of books and test papers in the Bond 11+ verbal reasoning range.

Mark your answers with an adult. Talk about the questions you got wrong or found hard to understand. Read the sections in this book again to help brush up on things you are still not sure about.

It is a good idea to go over examples of things that might come up in an 11+ verbal reasoning exam well before the date. A useful way to do this is to try some verbal reasoning tests that are similar to the exam you will be doing. The Bond Assessment Practice books and test papers, when used regularly, will provide useful, graded practice that will build your confidence and show you how well you cope with doing tests of this kind.

2. Time yourself

If you are just starting to prepare yourself, you may find it helpful to go through your first few Bond Assessment Papers in verbal reasoning untimed. This will help you to familiarise yourself with the types of questions and tasks you will face in the exam. Note down your scores (you could use the progress grids at the back of the Bond Assessment Practice books) and be sure to go over all the questions you found difficult until you understand them. After that, it is very important to give yourself a set time, just as you will have in the exam, so that you can practise pacing yourself and aiming to complete everything in the given time.

3. Revise strategies and techniques

It is also worth thinking about exam strategies and techniques. For many children, 11+ exams are the first exams they do in their lives, and they get very nervous at the thought of them. So do their parents! There are lots of hints on strategies and techniques in this book. Flick through them and talk about them to remind yourself. Highlight the ones that really work for you. It may be a good idea to make a reminder list of things to particularly look out for in the exam.

It is very important to remember that everyone is different. You will have your own way of coping and of doing things which may be quite different from the way other people work. If you have worked through this book, you will have a good idea of your own strengths and weaknesses, the things you find easy or difficult. You will have developed your own strategies and techniques in tests and in your learning.

4. Prepare for the exam day

"I'm so nervous..."

Of course you may be nervous, but actually many people find they can enjoy their exams if they feel confident and well prepared. After all, you will have done the practice; now it's your chance to show what you can do!

Just before the exam

Here are some useful things to remember before the exam day arrives and on the day itself:

- ✔ Don't worry about feeling a bit nervous; that's natural. Most children will feel anxious. Talk about your feelings and try to relax.
- ✔ Plan something fun to do after the exam is over.
- ✔ Try to have a good night's sleep.
- ✔ Eat a healthy breakfast and have something to drink.
- ✔ Make sure you have what you need: pencil/eraser/ruler/sharpener/tissues/glasses/water bottle/inhaler, etc.
- ✔ Get to the place where the exam is happening in plenty of time.
- ✔ Find out where the toilets are and go if you can before the exam starts.

In the exam room

There should be no distractions during the exam because everyone is in the same boat as you and there will be at least one adult making sure that everything runs smoothly. The adult will tell you when to start the exam and when to stop. It is also their job to keep an eye on everyone and ensure there is no cheating.

However, there will be some distractions no one can do anything about. It could be a new, strange environment. It's your first real, public exam – and everyone else's too. People have distracting habits, like rocking their chairs, dropping things, muttering, fidgeting, sniffing... Some people may have a cough or a cold. Someone may need to go to the toilet. A child may not realise you can't ask for help and put up their hand to ask a question. Someone may have finished ages before you and is staring out of the window. It can all be very distracting! What can you do? The best thing is to ignore everything in the exam room apart from the adult in charge, the clock, the times written on the board and the exam paper in front of you.

Here are some useful strategies and techniques to remember once you are in the exam room:

- ✔ Keep calm. If you get butterflies or feel anxious, sit up straight, make sure your shoulders are not hunched and take some deep breaths. This allows plenty of oxygen to get to your brain, which needs it!
- ✔ Think positive. You've done all the hard work preparing. Now enjoy yourself!
- ✔ Find the clock. Make sure you know where it is before you start, so you can do a time check during the exam.
- ✔ Read the question. Not doing so is the most common mistake and easy to do something about.
- ✔ Write your answers carefully. Again, most mistakes are careless ones.
- ✔ Show what you know. This is your big moment and what you've practised for. Try to enjoy showing what you have learnt.
- ✔ If you can't do a question, don't panic: have a go. Write something, and then put a mark in the margin, showing that you need to have another look if you have time at the end.
- ✔ Remember: a question left blank scores zero; a sensible guess may well be right.
- ✔ Leave time to check. Remember to leave a few minutes to check through your answers and make sure they make sense.
- ✔ Do your best: you can't do better than that!

GOOD LUCK!

Glossary

adjective – a word used to describe a **noun**.

adverb – a word usually used to describe a **verb**.

alternating sequence – where the numbers or letters do not increase or decrease in consecutive order.

anagram – a word made by rearranging the letters of another word.

analogy – a comparison between two things based on a similar feature or characteristic.

antonym – a word with an opposite meaning to another word.

association – a link or connection.

compound word – two or more words put together to make a new word.

consecutive – following one after another in a continuous series.

consonant(s) – a letter that is not a **vowel**.

context – the situation in which something happens and that helps you to understand it.

deduction – the process of using information you have in order to find the answer to a problem.

eliminate – to remove it completely.

equation – a number sentence with an equals sign (=). The left-hand sign has the same value as the right-hand side.

evaluate – to judge the quality, importance or value or something.

exception – something that does not follow common rules.

inverse operations – using the opposite of add subtract, divide and multiply to find missing numbers.

letter string – letters that commonly go together to make certain sounds.

logical – using sensible argument and thought.

noun – a naming word.

number bond – a pair of numbers that add together to give a bigger number.

prefix – a group of letters added in front of a **root word** to change its meaning.

pronunciation – how you say a word.

reasoning – the process of thinking about something in a **logical** way.

root word – the main part of a word to which **prefixes** and/or **suffixes** can be added.

statement – a sentence that is not a question or an exclamation.
substitution – to take the place of something or someone else.
suffix – a group of letters added after a **root word** to change its meaning.
synonym – a word with a similar meaning to another word.
value – a number that shows the result of a calculation.
verb – an action word that shows doing, having or being.
verbal – concerned with words only.
vocabulary – the range of words that a person knows and uses.
vowel(s) – any of the letters *a*, *e*, *i*, *o*, *u* and sometimes *y*.

Answers

1 Identify groups of words

1. Mouse and tiger belong in group A because they are animals.
   Piano and flute belong in group B because they are musical instruments.
   Coffee belongs in group C because it is a drink.
   Onion belongs in group D because it is a vegetable.
2. **a** river – lake, canal, ocean and river are all bodies of water.
   b glider – aeroplane, helicopter, jet and glider are all types of aircraft.
   c mug – plate, cup, bowl and mug are all types of crockery that we can use to eat or drink from.

2 Sort words into categories

1. Colours – beige, indigo and scarlet
   Metals – tin, steel and aluminium
   Insects – grasshopper, butterfly and earwig
2. Flowers – rose, tulip, orchid
   Hats – sombrero, fez, beret
   Animals – pangolin, leopard, ferret
3. Birds – eaglet, osprey, pheasant
   Vegetables – artichoke, fennel, broccoli
   Parts of the body – ankle, knuckle, pupil

3 Find words that do not belong

1. Easter, Friday – the other three are all months.
2. unicorn, dragon – the other three are real animals.
3. sword, castle – the other three all mean to guard against something.

4 Find words that have letters in common

1. Perceive is the only word that can be made.
2. Grudge can't be made because there is only one 'g' in underground.
3. items and times are the two words that contain the same letters.

5 Apply alphabetical order

1. The letter in ninth position is R.
2. The third word is surplus.
3. The fifth word is combust (tsubmoc).

6 Find letters that finish one word and begin the next

1. The letter is p – the words are grasp and people.
2. The letter is t – the words are sight, twist, start and trap.
3. The letters are el – the words are travel and electric.

7 Find a word hidden in a sentence

a polite as – the hidden word is teas.
b a blender – the hidden word is able.
c watch our – the hidden word is hour.
d toppled over – the hidden word is dove.

8 Add the missing letters to make a synonym of a given word

a The correct answer is D, pehs – the completed word is speechless.
b The correct answer is B, ugus – the completed word is courageous.
c The correct answer is E, intr – the completed word is sinister.

9 Add the missing letters to make an antonym of a given word

a The missing letters are e f c – the completed word is perfect.
b The missing letters are c l e a – the completed word is accidental.
c The missing letters are a i c l – the completed word is artificial.

10 Make new words by adding or removing letters

1. **a** w – the words are wing, wait, whale, wave.
   b k – the words are kite, known, knife, kettle.
2. **a** shore – add an r to shoe to make shore, which means beach.
   b crush – add a c to rush to make crush, which means squash.
3. **a** hunt – remove the u from haunt to leave hunt, which means search.
   b sale – remove the c from scale to leave sale, which means deal.

11 Move a letter to make new words

a c – the new words are rack and crumble.
b r – the new words are gill and trip.
c n – the new words are year and lend.
d t – the new words are sigh and stag.

12 Change letters to make new words

1 CAST – change the O to an A to make CAST and then the C to an F to make FAST.
2 a CLAP CLAY – change the I to an A to make CLAY, then change the P to a Y to make CLAY and finally change the C to a P to make PLAY.
  b SCARE SPARE – change the F to an E to make SCARE, then change the C to a P to make SPARE and finally change the R to a C to make SPACE.

13 Find the word that completes a word

a ROT – the complete word is **TROT**TED.
b SHE – the complete word is POLI**SHE**D.
c WAR – the complete word is **WAR**NED.
d ASK – the complete word is M**ASK**S.

14 Solve anagrams

1 The scrambled word is MEMORIES.
2 The scrambled words are SUDDENLY and BANG.
3 The scrambled word is ENERGY.
4 d – the scrambled words are FRIEND and SPIDERS.
5 l – the scrambled word is SCOWL.

15 Use a rule to create new words

1 audio – audio is the only word that contains four vowels (a, u ,i, o)
2 cash – change the last letter of the word from t to h.
3 calm – change the first letter of the second word in the pair to the next letter alphabetically, so b to c.
4 deck – rearrange letters 3, 4, 5, 6 in the order 6, 5, 3, 4.
5 lane – rearrange letters 2, 3, 5, 6 in the order 5, 2, 3, 6.
6 TRAP – the word uses letters 5, 6, 2, 1.
7 REAR – the word uses letters 4, 2, 6, 7.

16 Find words that are closest in meaning

1 divide, share – both of these mean to split something into parts.
2 attempt, try – both of these mean to have a go at doing something.
3 complain – grumble and complain both mean to protest about something.
4 beg, plead – both of these mean to ask for something in a desperate manner.
5 mend – mend means to repair something and rhymes with lend.

17 Find words that are opposite in meaning

1 definite – doubtful means unlikely, whereas definite means certain.
2 permit, forbid – permit means to allow, whereas forbid means prevent.
3 reckless, cautious – reckless means to be careless, whereas cautious means to be careful.

18 Find synonyms and antonyms

a endless, constant – both of these mean something that doesn't end.
b uncover, disclose, reveal – all of these mean show, whereas 'conceal' means hide.

19 Words with multiple meanings

a trip – trip can mean a journey or to tumble over.
b spot – spot can mean a smudge or to identify by sight.
c sink – sink means a place to wash or to fall downwards.

20 Combine two words to make a new word

1 a waterfall – waterfall is the only word that can be made.
  b passport – passport is the only word that can be made.
2 a nowhere – nowhere is the only word that can be made.
  b solid – solid is the only word that can be made.
3 a sea – the new words are seaweed, seashore, seashell, seagull.
  b book – the new words are bookmark, booklet, bookshop, bookcase.
  c wind – the new words are windscreen, windmill, windpipe, windsurf.

d ear – the new words are earphones, eardrum, earache, earring.
4 **a** break – the new words are heartbreak, daybreak, windbreak, outbreak, tiebreak.
  b nut – the new words are butternut, chestnut, peanut, hazelnut, doughnut.
  c light – the new words are firelight, headlight, spotlight, highlight, limelight.
  d less – the new words are powerless, countless, pointless, worthless, priceless.

21 Rearrange words to make a sentence

a dog, lady – the correct sentence is 'The kind lady adopted the stray dog.'
b divide, times – the correct sentence is 'How many times can you divide four into one hundred?'
c party, to – the correct sentence is 'Last weekend, I went to my grandmother's birthday party.'
d start, school – the correct sentence is 'What time does the school concert start this evening?'

22 Rearrange words to find an unnecessary word

a misty – the correct sentence is 'Rahul rescued the puppy from the deserted house.'
b leave – the correct sentence is 'The plants withered in the hot sun.'
c decide – the correct sentence is 'Politicians are elected by the people of the country.'

23 Select the best words to make a complete sentence

1 bake, oven, hours – the correct sentence is 'The recipe states that you need to bake the cake in the oven for two hours.'
2 replace 'television' with 'temperature' – the correct sentence is 'In winter, the average daily temperature is lower than it is in summer.'
3 trees – a forest, by definition, always has trees.

24 Complete word analogies

1 seven – seven completes the analogy because a pentagon is a five-sided shape and a heptagon is a seven-sided shape.

2 goose, gosling – goose and gosling complete the analogy because a cygnet is a young swan and a gosling is a young goose.
3 **a** wind, snow – wind and snow complete the analogy because a gale is a very strong wind and a blizzard is a severe snowstorm.
  b energetic, friendly – energetic and friendly complete the analogy because energetic is a synonym of lively and friendly is a synonym of sociable.

25 Code using numbers, letters and symbols

1 * % + ! $ – T = *, O = %, U = +, R = !, S = $
2 9165 – S = 9, A = 1, L = 6, E = 5
3 s b c x p – G = s, L = b, c = l, x = D, p = E
4 **a** SCARF – to get from the code to the word move each letter backwards by one.
  b KNVRU – to get from the word to the code move the letters in the sequence +1, –1, +1, –1, +1.

26 Logic problems

1 Maisie was late for school on Friday – If Maisie has to catch the 8 a.m. bus to get to school on time, then she must have been late for school on Friday because she caught a later bus. The other statements are either false or we don't have enough information to know if they are true or not.
2 Jacob – the order in which the children are seated from left to right is Arjun, Jacob, Amiya, Clare, Daisy, teacher.
3 Will – there are two certain facts: Jamie got 50 marks because he got half of the questions right and Will scored 64 correct answers. Saira got twenty more correct answers than Will so she scored 84. Saira's mark was six less than the winning result, therefore the highest score was 90, which was recorded by Zak. Finally, Megan scored 45 as her mark was half of Zak's. Therefore, the children are placed: 1st – Zak, 2nd – Saira, 3rd – Will, 4th – Jamie, 5th – Megan.
4 Carlos – Carlos does four activities (ice-skating, football, tennis and roller disco).

27 Letter-coded sums

a 35: 3 + 11 + 7 + 5 + 9 = 35
b K: 11 – 5 + 3 = 9   K = 9
c 99: 9 × 11 = 99
d 15: 9 ÷ 3 × 5 = 15

28 Complete the sum

a 6: 24 ÷ 3 = 6, 6 = 9 − 3
b 11: 8 × 7 = 56, 56 = 45 + 11
c 12: 21 − 11 = 6, 6 = 72 ÷ 12
d 5: 16 ÷ 2 + 7 = 15, 15 = 3 + 7 − 5
e 4: 7 × 6 − 10 = 32, 32 = 8 × 4

29 Related numbers

1 26 – Add the two outside numbers (14 + 12 = 26).
2 9 – Divide the first number by the third number (108 ÷ 12 = 9).
3 24 – Add the outside numbers together (11 + 1 = 12). Double the answer (12 × 2 = 24).
4 3 – Subtract the third number from the first number (11 − 6 = 5). Subtract 2 (5 − 2 = 3).

30 Number sequences

1 a 48, 96 – Double the number each time.
   b 20, 27 – The number added increases by 1 each time: + 3, + 4, + 5, + 6, + 7.
   c 32, 24 – Subtract 8 each time.
2 a 12, 5 – There are two sequences that alternate. In the first sequence, add 2 each time. In the second sequence, subtract 5 each time.
   b 21, 4 – There are two sequences that alternate. In the first sequence, add 4 each time. In the second sequence, subtract 1 each time.
   c 7, 2 – There are two sequences that alternate. In the first sequence, subtract 3 each time. In the second sequence, divide by 2 each time.

31 Letter sequences

1 V U – both letters move back by one each time.
2 K P, P K – the first letter moves forward one additional letter each time, + 1, + 2, + 3, and so on. The second letter moves back by one additional letter each time, − 1, − 2, − 3, and so on.
3 W X, A Z – There are two sequences that alternate. The first sequence moves forward two letters each time. The second sequence moves back by two letters each time.

32 Letter analogies

1 Q P – each letter in the pair moves back two letters.
2 S D – the first letter in the pair moves back four letters, the second letter moves forward two letters.
3 G B – the first letter in the pair moves back five letters, the second letter moves forward four letters.
4 X 7 – the letter in the pair moves back five letters, the number adds five.

33 Complete crosswords

a

Y	E	A	R	S
		P		Y
P	A	P	E	R
		L		U
S	H	E	E	P

b

M	E	T	E	R
A		H		I
R	E	E	L	S
S		I		E
H	E	R	O	N

c

	O		C		A
A	B	S	O	R	B
	T		M		R
B	U	R	E	A	U
	S		T		P
B	E	D	S	I	T

OXFORD
UNIVERSITY PRESS

Great Clarendon Street, Oxford, OX2 6DP, United Kingdom

Oxford University Press is a department of the University of Oxford.
It furthers the University's objective of excellence in research, scholarship,
and education by publishing worldwide. Oxford is a registered trade mark
of Oxford University Press in the UK and in certain other countries

Text © Alison Primrose 2024
© Oxford University Press 2024

The moral rights of the author have been asserted
Database right Oxford University Press (maker)

First published in 2024

All rights reserved. No part of this publication may be reproduced,
stored in a retrieval system, or transmitted, used for text and data mining,
or used for training artificial intelligence, in any form or by any means,
without the prior permission in writing of Oxford University Press,
or as expressly permitted by law, or under terms agreed with the appropriate
reprographics rights organization. Enquiries concerning reproduction
outside the scope of the above should be sent to the Rights Department,
Oxford University Press, at the address above

You must not circulate this book in any other binding or cover
and you must impose this same condition on any acquirer

British Library Cataloguing in Publication Data
Data available

ISBN: 9781382054218

10 9 8 7 6 5 4 3 2 1

Printed in the UK

The manufacturing process conforms to the environmental regulations
of the country of origin

Acknowledgements

The Publishers would like to thank Sue Rowe for the material
she contributed to this edition.

Cover illustrations by Lo Cole
Typeset by Integra